Collins
30
minute

Acrylics

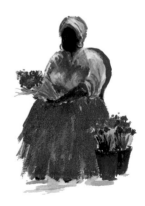

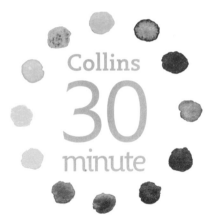

Collins

30

minute

Acrylics

Soraya French

First published in 2007 by
Collins, an imprint of
HarperCollins*Publishers*
77-85 Fulham Palace Road
Hammersmith, London W6 8JB

www.collins.co.uk

12 11 10 09 08 07
8 7 6 5 4 3 2 1

Editor: Diana Vowles
Designer: Kathryn Gammon

ISBN 978 0 00 725650 1

Colour reproduction by Colourscan, Singapore
Printed and bound by Printing Express, Hong Kong

Page 2: **Caribbean Sea,** 30 × 36 cm (12 × 14 in)

About the Author

Soraya French was born in Tehran and came to England
in 1977. Now a full-time professional artist, she is a
demonstrator for Daler-Rowney, runs private art workshops,
regularly demonstrates her
painting techniques to art
groups and widely exhibits her
work. Soraya is a member of
the Society of Floral Painters,
and is President of the Andover
Art Society. She is a contributor
to *The Artist* magazine and in
July 2005 was the winner of
the SAA Artist of the Year
award. For more information,
visit www.sorayafrench.com

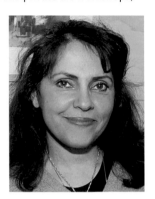

Dedication
To Tim, my husband and best friend, whose selfless love, help and
encouragement have enabled me to follow my dream.

Acknowledgements
My thanks to Caroline Churton, without whose patient help and guidance
this book wouldn't have come to fruition; to Diana Vowles, for hours of
editing and all the encouraging emails; to Kathryn Gammon for her fantastic
design work; to Tracy Mason of Daler-Rowney, and to Sally Bulgin and
Caroline Griffiths of *The Artist* magazine for believing in me. My grateful
thanks to my tutor, Richard Plincke, for his influence in the way that I
perceive art, and also my wonderful teacher, Geoff Crabb, who has so
generously fortified me with his vast knowledge and wisdom over the years.
Finally, to my two lovely children, Yasmin and Saasha, for their love and
understanding, and most of all to my father-in-law, Roy French, for
encouraging me to pursue my painting.

CONTENTS

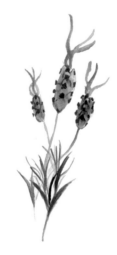

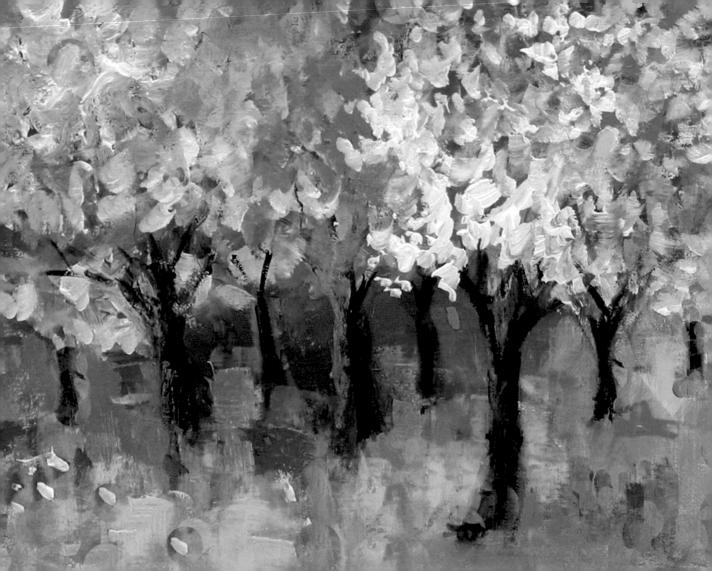

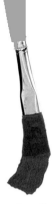

INTRODUCTION

Acrylic paint is by far the most versatile medium available for the artist today. Water-based, it can be used like watercolour but also offers opacity that makes it especially suitable for the beginner. At the same time, more experienced and experimental artists can take advantage of the unique characteristics of the medium and push the boundaries to express and develop their ideas.

Within the pages of this book, you will be able to find all you need to get you started on your journey of exploring this fantastic medium – and you'll discover the possibilities of what you can achieve with your paints in just 30 minutes.

◀ **Cherry Blossoms**
18 × 23 cm (7 × 9 in)
This painting is a good example of using the heavy texture and vibrancy of acrylic colours to maximum effect.

The advantages of acrylics

Acrylics are an odourless, quick-drying, flexible medium that can mimic both watercolour and oil colours. However, they also have some unique qualities of their own. The opacity of acrylic pigments enables the artist to cover or rectify mistakes, making them ideal for beginners; they can be applied with brushes or a painting knife; they can be used on a multitude of different surfaces; they dry fast so that a quick succession of washes and layers can be applied easily; and while water is perfect for diluting them, there is also a whole range of mediums and additives that can modify them.

Consequently, acrylics offer the artist numerous possibilities for experimenting with different techniques of application and creating exciting effects with texture. They are also one of the most durable and permanent mediums available.

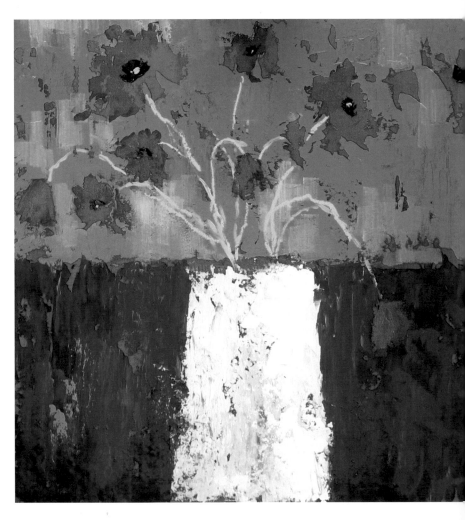

▶ **Poppies on Blue**
30 × 30 cm (12 × 12 in)
In this picture the poppies were scraped over the blue background with a painting knife.

The aim of this book

Many people lead such busy lives today that the idea of a time-consuming leisure activity, however pleasurable, can be offputting. The aim of *30-minute Acrylics* is to give you concise information and quick exercises so that you can take up painting without having to invest a huge amount of time. Acrylics are the ideal medium, as there is very little preparation required and you can be as spontaneous as you wish.

I hope that after trying a few of the exercises you will share my enthusiasm for this amazing medium – and you may even realize that this is the start of a lifelong pursuit.

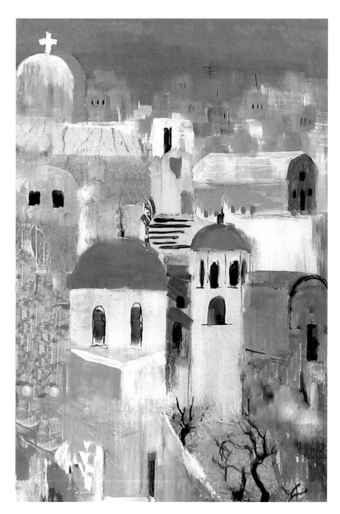

▶ **Mediterranean Buildings**
(detail)
A combination of collage, ink and heavy body colour provided the texture for this painting.

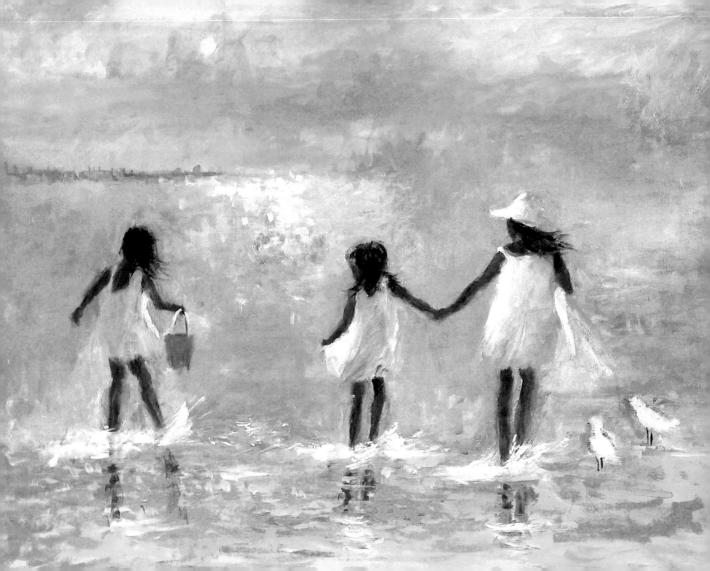

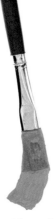

ESSENTIAL EQUIPMENT

The wide range of art materials available to the artist today can sometimes be more of a hindrance than a help. The variety of consistencies in acrylic colour can make the choice confusing for the beginner, but the exercises in this book will help you to make the right choice for a particular subject or technique. In this chapter you will find details of all the basic equipment you need to get started – paints, brushes, supports and accessories.

While they are more expensive, I cannot emphasize too highly the importance of investing in good-quality artist's materials, which go a long way to ensure your progress and enjoyment of painting.

◀ **Children on the Beach**
40 × 51 cm (16 × 20 in)
Here I used both transparent and opaque colours, with Titanium White for the light areas.

Acrylic colours

Acrylic colours come in different consistencies, and which you select will depend upon your individual style and subject matter. The various types can intermix, giving you a further range of choice. Within the categories below, the consistency varies from manufacturer to manufacturer, as do the colours, even if the name may be the same.

Soft body

Otherwise known as flow formula, this paint is heavier than acrylic ink but has a runny consistency and is more suitable for the watercolourist. It can be thickened by using impasto gel. An example is Daler-Rowney System 3 colours, available in tubes and larger pots.

Heavy body

These colours, such as the Daler-Rowney Cryla range, are more full-bodied and can be thinned to use in watercolour style or applied thick like oil paints. However, you would still need to thicken them further for heavily textured styles.

Super heavy body

Formulated to create heavy textures and to retain brush strokes, these acrylics have a more buttery consistency, but can still be thinned down if you need to glaze with them. The Daler-Rowney System 3D range comes in large tubes.

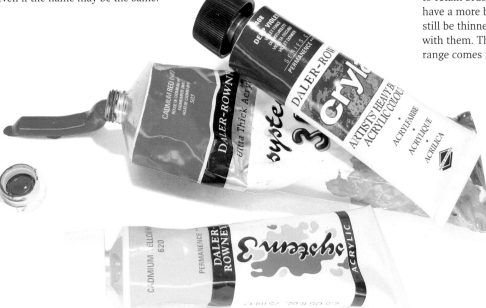

◀ Soft body, heavy body and super heavy body acrylic paints give the artist varying consistencies to work with.

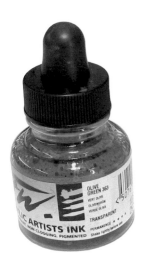

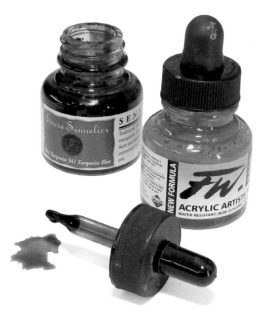

Mediums and additives

While you can dilute acrylics with water, there are also mat and gloss mediums which can be used with acrylic colours in order to improve flow and increase transparency. They are particularly useful in glazing technique.

Also available are chemicals that are added to change the nature of the paint, such as slow-drying medium, which lengthens the drying time. These should be used sparingly.

Inks

Acrylic inks are the most fluid form of acrylic colours. They are highly suitable for watercolour techniques but have the advantage of drying to a waterproof film which cannot be disturbed once dry, with the consequence that there is less likelihood of muddy colours.

The inks are fabulously vibrant and highly permanent. They can be used on their own or combined with thick colour, and can also be applied as glaze over thick colour at the latter stages of a painting. They come in small bottles with a useful dropper.

▲ Available in both brilliant and subtle colours, acrylic inks are invaluable for their versatility and permanence.

QUICK TIP

Have a separate watercolour-type palette for the inks and keep a well for each colour as remaining stains may affect new colours.

Brushes

Invest in a set of good-quality synthetic watercolour and acrylic brushes, the former to use with the inks and the latter, which have stiffer hair, for the opaque techniques. The size of your brushes depends on the size of your paintings, but a 25mm (1 in) one-stroke wash brush, a short flat No. 12 acrylic brush for covering larger areas and a selection of smaller round brushes and flat brushes will suit most artists. Riggers in both the watercolour and acrylic range will also be useful.

Palettes

Acrylic paints dry to a plastic film, so it is important to keep them wet during a painting session. A stay-wet palette comprises a tray, two layers of paper (absorbent and tissue) and a lid. Both layers should be dampened to make a surface to mix paints on. You can also spray the paints from time to time to keep them workable during a painting session.

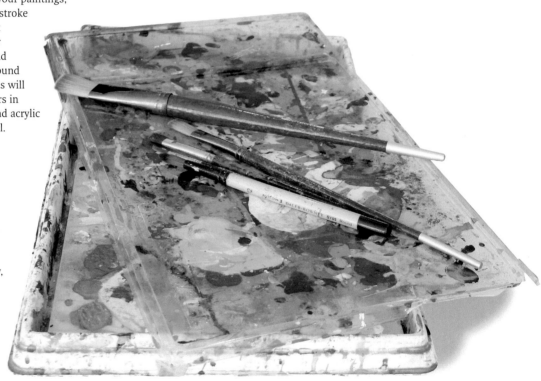

▼ With a damp surface to mix colours on and a lid to keep the moisture in, a stay-wet palette helps to keep the paints workable for a longer period.

Supports

Acrylics are so versatile it is easier to say which surfaces you cannot paint on rather than list those on which you can. Oil-based and shiny surfaces are unsuitable as the colour will peel off at a later stage. However, you can use all types of watercolour paper, acrylic paper, mountboard and many types of canvases.

Gesso

Acrylic gesso is a primer that is used to prepare the surface prior to painting. This is optional when you use watercolour paper, acrylic paper or mountboard, but should be used on MDF (medium-density fibreboard). Gesso is available in both white and black.

Other equipment

You will also need a comfortable easel or table easel, a painting board, water pots, masking tape and kitchen towels. A painting knife is also useful.

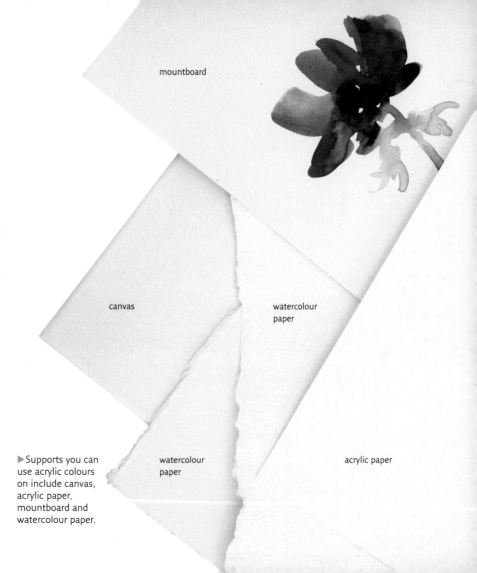

mountboard

canvas

watercolour paper

watercolour paper

acrylic paper

▶ Supports you can use acrylic colours on include canvas, acrylic paper, mountboard and watercolour paper.

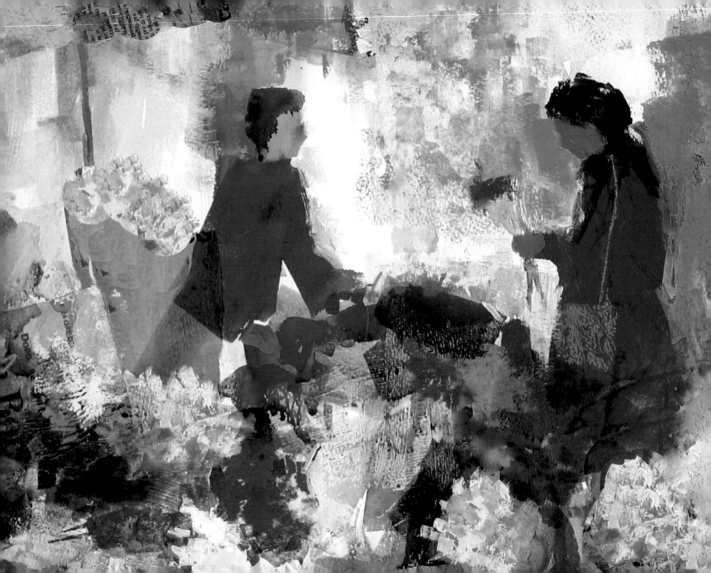

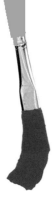

COLOUR AND TONE

Colour is the most exciting aspect of painting and the very first element that will evoke an emotional response from the viewer. It is absolutely crucial for the beginner to invest some time in grasping a basic understanding of colour and its three components – hue, saturation and value.

Hue refers to the name of the colour, such as red, blue and yellow, while saturation is the brightness or dullness of the colour and value is its lightness or darkness. This chapter explores all these aspects and gives you exercises that will help you to learn to mix and use your colours quickly and confidently.

◀ **Flower Stall**
28 × 38 cm (11 × 15 in)
This picture is about colour balance and harmony. Neutral tones create the structure and bright colours add zest.

A basic palette

Successful colour mixing in acrylics can be achieved with a relatively limited number of colours that mix to create an infinite number of secondary and tertiary colours, tints and neutrals.

My suggested basic colour palette is: Titanium White, Yellow Ochre, Burnt Sienna, Ultramarine, Lemon Yellow, Crimson Alizarin (Hue), Phthalo Blue, Cadmium Yellow and Cadmium Red.

Titanium White is a very important colour in acrylic painting. As you progress you may wish to add some extra colours to your palette, such as Magenta for flowers, Coeruleum for skies, Dioxazine Purple, a lovely dark purple useful for creating dark undertones, and Payne's Grey, a versatile dark colour.

As you gain experience you will create your own voice and unique colour palette and your work will become recognizable through this.

Magenta

Coeruleum

Dioxazine Purple

Payne's Grey

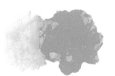

Titanium White

Yellow Ochre

Burnt Sienna

Ultramarine

Lemon Yellow

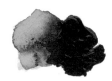

Crimson Alizarin (Hue)

Phthalo Blue

Cadmium Yellow

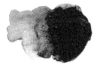

Cadmium Red

QUICK TIP

Use Payne's Grey in moderation – it is made of two or three colours and should not be mixed with more than one other colour. Mixed with Lemon Yellow, it makes a useful green.

Primary colours

The three colours of red, yellow and blue on the colour wheel are known as the primary colours. These cannot be created by mixing other colours, but they do have variations within them such as a purple-red or an orange-red.

Secondary colours

Secondary colours are made by mixing the two adjacent primary colours on the colour wheel. Red and blue make purple; red and yellow make orange; and yellow and blue make green.

To mix vibrant purple, orange and green, you should mix the two primaries biased towards the same colour. For example, the purple-biased Ultramarine blue with purple-biased Crimson Alizarin (Hue) make vibrant purple, whereas Phthalo Blue (Green Shade) and Cadmium Red, which has an orange bias, make a greyish purple.

Tertiary colours

Mixing a primary and a secondary colour will produce what is known as a tertiary colour. For example, yellow added to orange makes a yellow-orange.

Complementary colours

Complementary colours are contrasting colours situated opposite each other on a typical colour wheel, such as red and green, blue and orange, and yellow and purple. They play an important role in painting. Placed next to each other, they make dazzling and vibrant contrasts. They can also be used to modify or knock back one another – for example, a bright yellow can be dulled by adding a touch of purple.

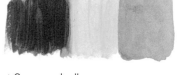

▲ Orange and yellow mixed together make yellow-orange, which is a tertiary colour.

▼ **Clementine on Blue Cloth**
In this example of complementary colours, the orange placed against the blue creates a lovely contrast.

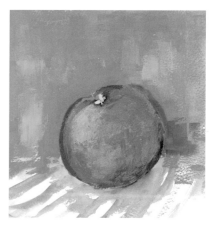

◀ Red, blue and yellow are the primary colours.

▶ Yellow and blue mixed together make green, a secondary colour. Yellow and red make orange, and red and blue make purple.

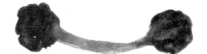

Neutrals and tints

Neutral tones and tints are just as important as the more vibrant colours. In a painting of predominantly vivid colours the neutrals have the supporting roles; without them the painting may look too bright and garish.

Mixing neutrals

Neutrals are the hues that are not on the colour wheel, such as black and white, grey, brown and beige. Neutral greys are made by mixing complementary colours in different proportions. By varying the proportion of the individual colours used in the mix you can achieve cooler or warmer versions of neutral colours. Greys mixed in this way are much more exciting than those made by mixing black and white. Browns, which are also referred to as earth colours, are made by mixing the three primaries together.

Remember that colours exist in relation to each other; a colour which may look dull and muted next to a vivid colour may look quite bright when placed next to an even more muted colour, so what you mixed on your palette may look different once you have placed it in context in your painting.

Making tints

Bright acrylic colours can be made into beautiful subtle tones by adding white. These paler and more delicate shades are known as tints, and mixing primary, secondary and tertiary colours with varying degrees of white will give you an infinite number of them.

| QUICK TIP

Mixing your neutrals by using the colours that already appear in your painting makes a more harmonious piece of work.

▶ Ultramarine and Burnt Sienna mix to a lovely grey.

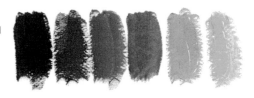

▶ Adding white to red has created pink, which is a tint of red.

▶ For a warm grey, mix Coeruleum with Lemon Yellow and a touch of Magenta.

Colour temperature

Reds, yellows and oranges are usually thought of as warm colours, while blues, greens and purples are cool. However, there are also warm and cool versions within each group. For example, Cadmium Yellow is a warm yellow as it is biased towards orange and Lemon Yellow is a cooler yellow, biased towards green; Coeruleum is a cool green-biased blue, whereas Ultramarine is a warm blue biased towards violet.

Cool colours recede while warm colours advance, so understanding colour temperature will help you to create depth and recession in your landscape paintings. This doesn't mean that you shouldn't paint a red or yellow field in the distance, but modifying the colours to make them appear cooler will set them back in the landscape. In secondary colours, the proportion of each individual primary that is used will determine the colour temperature. For example, you can make a green appear cooler by adding more blue or make it warmer by adding more yellow.

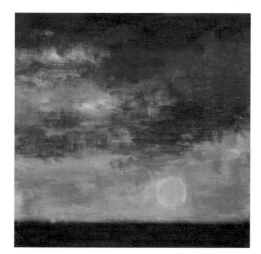

◀ **Sunset Study**
The cooler reds and yellows of this sunset are high in the sky; lower down, as it nears the horizon, the sky gets warmer with oranges and bright yellows.

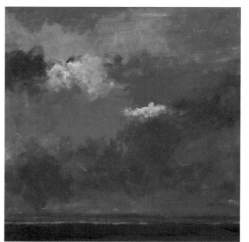

◀ **Sky Study**
This study shows warm and cool colours within the blue spectrum. Note that the sky gets warmer nearer the horizon.

▌QUICK TIP

You can knock back an area of warm tone by glazing it with a cooler colour.

Using colour temperature

This painting shows how the use of cool and warm colours in a landscape gives the composition a feeling of recession, echoing the phenomenon of aerial perspective which causes colours to fade into blues and greys as we look into the far distance.

MATERIALS USED

Short flat brushes
  Nos 4, 8; round
  brushes Nos 6, 8;
  rigger No. 6
Mountboard
Burnt Sienna
Cadmium Orange
Cadmium Yellow

Coeruleum
Flame Red ink
Lemon Yellow
Light Blue Violet
Phthalo Blue (Green
  Shade)
Titanium White
Yellow Ochre

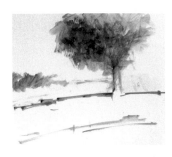

1 Using Burnt Sienna, loosely map out the main structure of the painting. Notice how the horizontal shapes are balanced by the verticals of the trees.

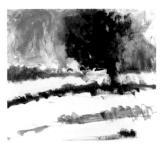

2 Block in the dark tones and apply cool blue to the far trees. Lay a wash of Light Blue Violet over the sky. Paint the distant land Lemon Yellow and apply warmer orange-yellow to the foreground.

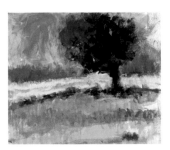

3 Next paint the distant trees with a layer of Light Blue Violet to make them recede and bring much warmer yellow and orange into the foreground. Apply warmer green to the tips of the foliage on the tree.

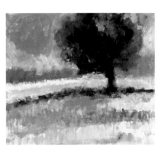

4 Paint the top half of the sky with Coeruleum and gradually add the warmer Light Blue Violet closer to the horizon. In the distance, add cooler blue-green to the foliage and the meadow.

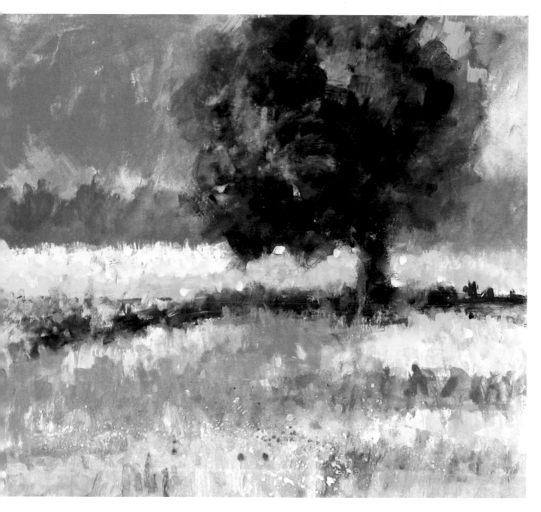

5 Make all the foreground colours stronger, thicker and warmer to bring them further forward. Add more Burnt Sienna to the tree trunk and shape the foliage. Emphasize the cooler greens in the distance, then bring some cooler colours into the shadow areas in the foreground. Finally, splatter a little white and red to suggest summer flowers.

◀ **Summer Landscape**
25 × 28 cm (10 × 11 in)

Tonal values

The tonal value of a colour refers to its lightness or darkness. However, within individual colours this is a relative concept and the best way to grasp it is to compare the colour against the grey scale below, which shows black right up to white with all the shades of grey in between. For example, yellow at its highest saturation (darkest value) only compares to a light grey, whereas blue at its darkest value is comparable to a dark grey.

Tonal value is one of the most important design elements in a painting. When you are making a representational painting, to create a dynamic image it is crucial not only to use the right local colour of an object (for example a yellow banana) but also to use it at its correct value within the painting, which gives objects their dimension. Make light against dark against light your mantra; a painting that lacks tonal structure appears flat and lifeless, which in turn makes it not only boring but most of all unconvincing to the eye.

▲ This little exercise shows the value of colours against their grey value. Yellow at its highest intensity compares to the lightest grey, while blue at its highest intensity compares to a dark grey and crimson to a mid-grey.

▼ To assess the tonal value of a colour you can compare it to this nine-step grey value scale.

QUICK TIP

One of the best ways to judge the tonal value of your subject matter is to look at it through half-closed eyes.

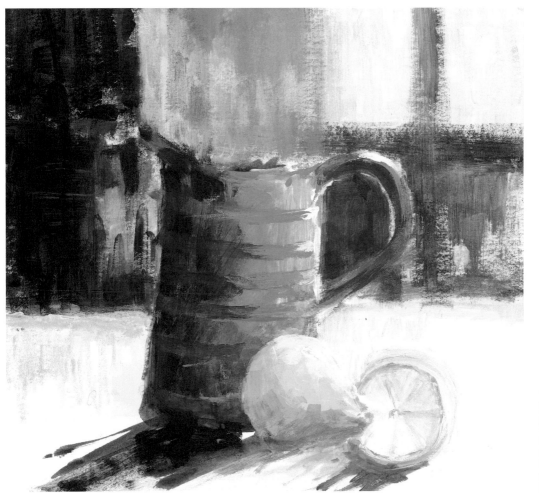

◄ **Still Life
with Lemon**
25 × 25 cm (10 × 10 in)
This backlit still life
shows how the
direction of light
affects the tonal
value of each object's
local colour.

Working in monochrome

It is often much easier to establish tonal values when you are working with pencils or charcoal – in other words, in black and white. Things can go slightly awry when colour comes into the equation and confusion can set in. A good way of getting to grips with introducing the correct values when you are working in colour is to practise by painting monochromes – that is, painting the subject with a single colour, in its different tonal values.

It is amazing how removing the worry of an extended colour palette allows you to concentrate on shape, form and the correct tonal value and to start making convincing pictures. In time this can be translated into colour by comparing the local colour of the elements in your painting against a grey scale to assess the correct tone. Remember to look at your subject through half-closed eyes, as this will reduce the details and break down the subject into light and dark values. With practice, this will become effortless and instinctive.

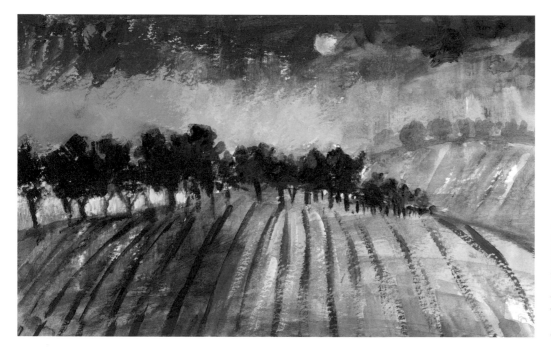

◄ **Moonlit Fields**
16 × 27 cm (6½ × 10½ in)
I used Dioxazine Purple to do this little study. It was so much easier to judge the tonal values within the subject matter using just one colour.

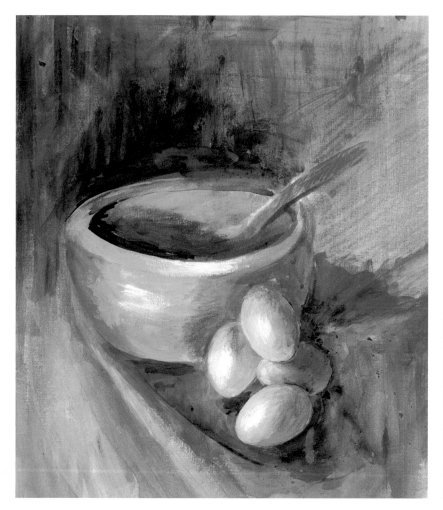

◀ **Kitchen Still Life**
33 × 25 cm (13 × 10 in)
This still life was
done in Sepia plus
white and shows
light, dark and mid
tones. The subject
was lit from the
left-hand side.

QUICK OVERVIEW

☐ Organize a basic colour palette and
become familiar with it.

☐ Mix neutral greys from complementary
colours, not black and white.

☐ Use warm and cool colours to give
depth to your pictures.

☐ Check the tonal values in your painting.

☐ Practise painting in monochrome.

Tonal values

To create a three-dimensional object, you need to depict it using the correct tonal values of its local colour. No matter how beautifully you paint the elements within your picture, without the right tonal structure it won't convince the viewer and will become flat and one-dimensional.

Make a grey scale
Paint a nine-step grey scale (see page 24), starting with black and all the shades of grey right up to white. You can then compare the tonal values of your colours against their equal value on the grey scale. Through practice and experience you will become able to judge the correct tonal values instinctively.

Paint a still life
Arrange a simple still life and light it with a spotlight from one direction so that you have a dramatic contrast between the lights and darks. Block in your lights, darks and mid-tones without any outlines around the objects so that they are separated tonally. Place light against dark against light throughout the composition. If you find it difficult, start by painting it in monochrome.

Repeat the same exercise, placing a still life on a table in the garden on a sunny day so that some objects are lit and some are in shadow. This time you will have less control over light and shade, so make a considered tonal study before going on to paint the scene in colour. As the light will change rapidly it is also a good idea to make notes about light on your sketch and perhaps take a photograph to refer to later.

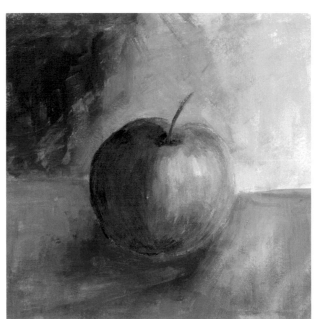

◀ **Tonal Study with Apple**
20 × 23 cm (8 × 9 in)
This little study of an apple shows how the roundness of the fruit has been achieved by changing the tone. Directional light can create interest and drama in a painting.

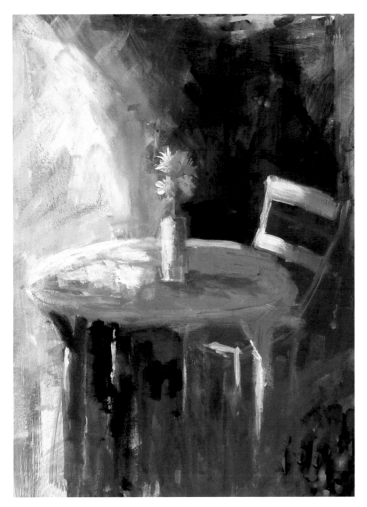

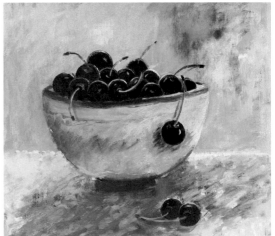

◀ **Garden Corner**
30 × 25 cm (12 × 10 in)
This painting shows the different tones within a white object. Even though the object is white, you only see it as such where it has been flooded with light.

▲ **Bowl of Cherries**
20 × 25 cm (8 × 10 in)
In this picture you can see how the round shapes of the cherries have been represented by the change in the tonal value of their local colour, which is a deep magenta. Changes in the tonal value also separate each cherry from the one next to it.

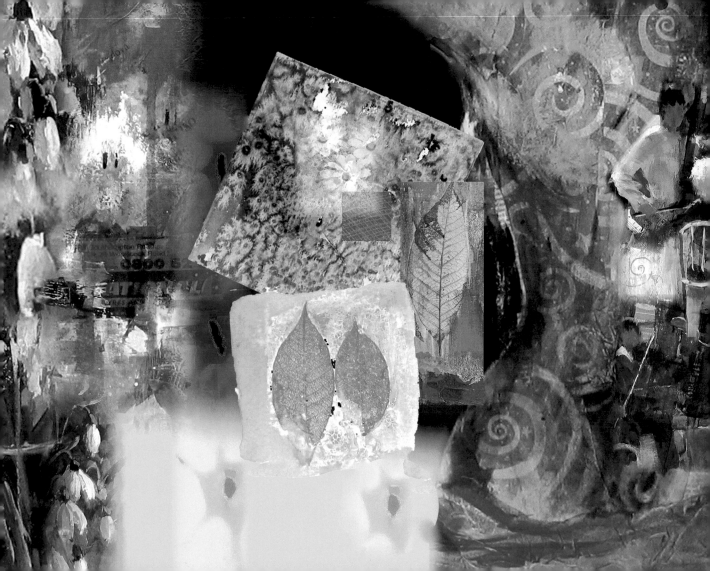

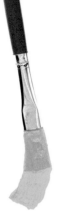

TECHNIQUES

Technique refers to the craft aspect of painting as opposed to the aesthetics, and it can be learnt through sheer hard work and practice. The versatility of acrylic colours creates scope for a wide range of effective and exciting methods of applying them to various surfaces. You can dilute and use the pigments with watercolour techniques such as wet-into-wet or employ opaque techniques such as impasto style or scumbling.

This chapter introduces a variety of these techniques, which can be used singly or in combination in your paintings. None is laborious, and you'll be able to create pictures in a short space of time.

◀ **Medley**
29 × 42 cm (11 × 16½ in)
The collage shown here is composed of a few of my paintings using techniques described within this chapter.

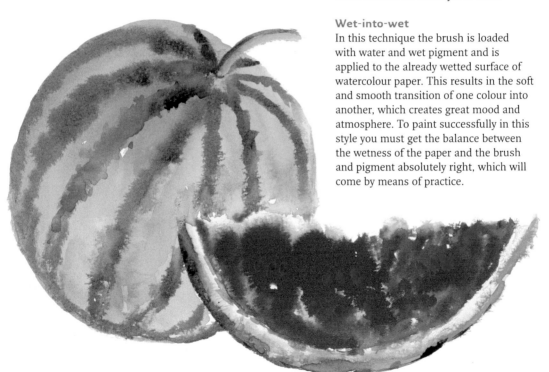

Watercolour technique

Acrylic colours can be diluted and applied in the style of watercolour washes. Acrylic inks and soft body colours are most suitable for this style of work.

Wet-into-wet

In this technique the brush is loaded with water and wet pigment and is applied to the already wetted surface of watercolour paper. This results in the soft and smooth transition of one colour into another, which creates great mood and atmosphere. To paint successfully in this style you must get the balance between the wetness of the paper and the brush and pigment absolutely right, which will come by means of practice.

◄ **Watermelons**
I applied Dark Green ink to wet paper to shape the skin of the watermelon. I rewetted the area of fruit and when I applied red ink all the colours ran and fused together. While the paint was still wet I put in the seeds with Payne's Grey.

QUICK TIP

For a smooth transition of paint wet-into-wet, load the brush and drop colour onto the wet surface rather than brushing it on.

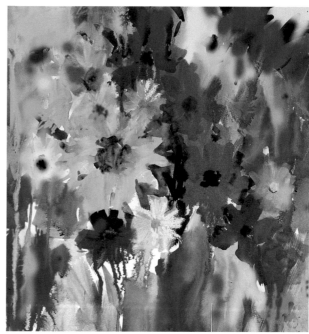

▲ **Sunflower**
I dropped Bright Yellow ink onto wet paper to form the petals of this sunflower. Once this had dried, I rewetted the centre of the flower and painted the shape of the centre with a mixture of Bright Yellow and Purple Lake ink.

▶ **Flower Fusion**
40 × 38 cm (16 × 15 in)
After wetting the paper, I applied washes of colour to each flowerhead. Once these had dried, I pulled the painting together by shaping some of the petals and applying more washes of ink.

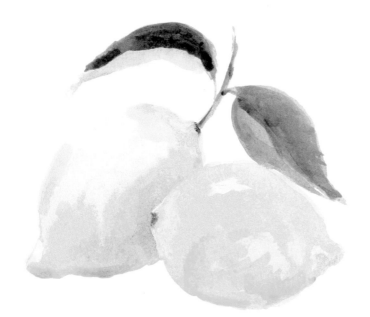

◀ **Lemons**
I painted the lemons with Lemon Yellow, with Bright Yellow for the darker shadow areas and diluted Indigo behind the front lemon as shadow colour. The leaves and the stem were painted in Olive Green, with Indigo added to the darker areas of the leaves.

▼ **Little Sailor**
30 × 20 cm (12 × 8 in)
My first step was to apply a wash of Indigo on the paper, saving white paper for the boat and sail. I added yellow which mixed with the Indigo on paper to suggest the green of the bushes. Finally I put some shadow on the boat and sail.

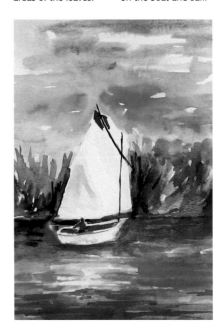

Wet-on-dry

Wet-on-dry is one of the most common ways of using water-based media. In this method, wet paint is applied onto dry paper or another layer of dry paint. This technique creates hard edges. It can also be used in combination with wet-into-wet technique if a painting requires both soft and hard edges. An acrylic wash of colour becomes waterproof once it is dry, so the subsequent washes do not disturb each other and colours retain their vibrancy.

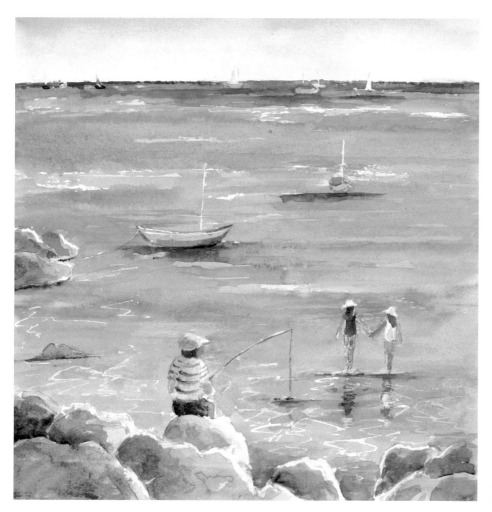

◄ **Children Fishing**
30 × 30 cm (12 × 12 in)
I applied Coeruleum
with touches of
Lemon Yellow in the
sea area. The rocks
and the boats were
painted with washes
of Yellow Ochre
and Burnt Sienna,
building up the
colour from light to
darker washes.

Opaque technique

It is great to take advantage of the heavy body quality of acrylic colours to paint in a variety of styles similar to oil painting without the problem of the lengthy drying time that oil pigments need. This is an ideal method for a beginner as mistakes can be easily rectified.

Impasto style

Applying thick colour with either a brush or a painting knife so that it lies in a slightly raised manner is known as impasto. Acrylic colours are highly suitable for this way of painting as they dry rapidly, allowing further application of colour in quick succession.

Heavier body acrylic colours are best for impasto as they retain the brush marks. Alternatively, you can add impasto gel or other bulking material to the thinner paints to make them suitable for impasto application. A third option is to use either texture gel or modelling paste to make a textured surface before applying any colour.

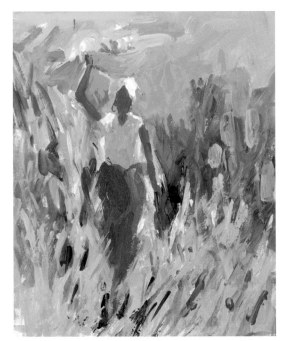

◄ **Walking Through the Field**
27 × 24 cm (10½ × 9½ in)
Thick colour has retained the brush marks and helps to create movement in this swift and spontaneous painting.

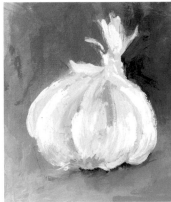

▶ **Garlic**
38 × 38 cm (14 × 14 in)
Super-heavy body Titanium White and a dab of purple were used to give the garlic its bulbous shape and texture.

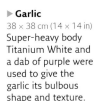

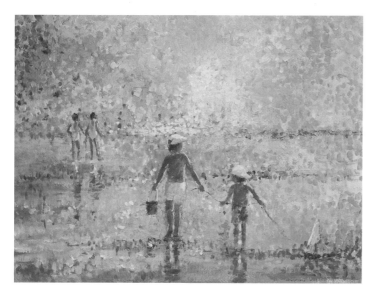

Keep your brushes in water during the painting session. Clean them frequently to keep colours fresh and vibrant.

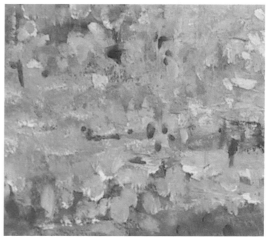

Broken colour

Applying pigment in a way that allows some of the colours from the layer beneath to show through is an effective way of painting. You can either brush almost dry pigment over a base colour or use dabs of colour, leaving the base layer partly visible.

For maximum effect with this method, use complementary colours and take advantage of the fact that when the dabs of primary colour are juxtaposed they will appear from a distance to be their secondary colour.

▲ **Midday Sun**
40 × 51 cm (16 × 20 in)
The complementary colours yellow and purple, applied in dabs, create a good contrast in this painting. The whole colour scheme was designed to create harmony.

▲ This detail of *Midday Sun* shows how the Yellow Ochre used as a base colour can be seen through the final layers.

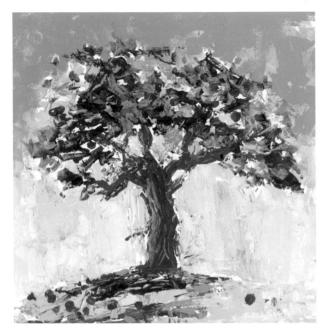

Using a painting knife

Applying paint with a painting knife is a tactile and enjoyable way of working. The marks made are quite different from those of a brush and the effects are much more random and less stylized, making it easier to create semi-abstract images.

To achieve this technique successfully you need the heavier body acrylic colours, and super heavy body acrylics are even better. Depending upon the shape of your painting knife, you can use long, sweeping strokes or shorter, more controlled marks. You can scratch into the thick paint and create texture at the same time.

▼ Vary the type of marks you make to create a more interesting image.

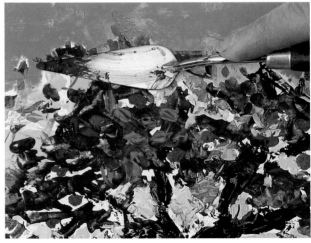

▲ **Apple Tree**
23 × 23 cm (9 × 9 in)
I painted the bark with Burnt Umber, then applied a mixture of dark and light green for the foliage and the grass in the foreground. Once these layers had dried I added the apples in dabs of bright red.

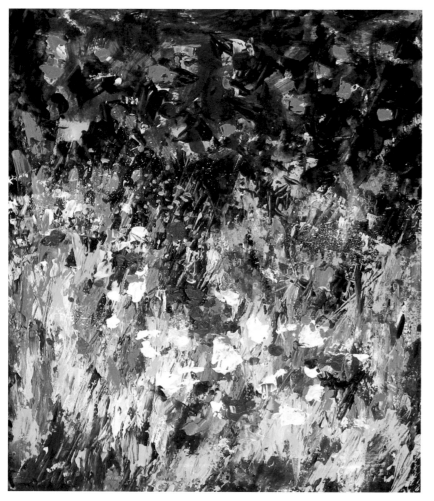

◄ **Flower Field**
30 × 27 cm (12 × 10½ in)
I laid a layer of dark green over the background trees and made a diagonal pattern of dark colours in the foreground. Once that had dried, I applied thick layers of lime green, white, light blue and magenta in dabs of colour to suggest the flower meadow.

▲ In this detail of *Flower Field* you can see how I have scratched into the paint to suggest the stems.

Combining transparent and opaque colours

Using a combination of transparent and opaque colours is one of the most rewarding ways in which to paint with acrylics. Transparent washes of colour in either acrylic ink or diluted tube colour provide translucent passages in the painting which create depth and recession, while the thicker application of colour can provide textural effects. Transparent colours can also be used at the later stages to glaze an area for a change of colour and tonal values. The marriage of the two makes for a more rounded and interesting painting than one where only a single paint quality is used.

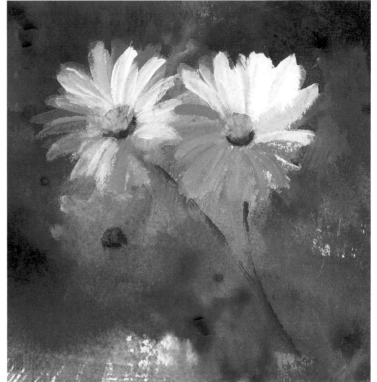

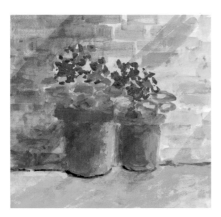

◀ **Geraniums**
Here I used opaque paint first and then applied transparent glazes as cast shadow to give a sunny feel.

▲ **Daisies**
15 × 15 cm (6 × 6 in)
In this painting of daisies the transparent colours set the scene with the dark background.

I painted the daisies in heavier-textured Titanium White where the light hits them and used light grey where they are in shadow.

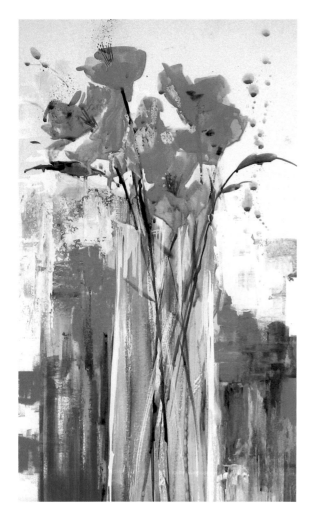

◀ **Lilies in Tall Vase**
48 × 30 cm (19 × 12 in)
In this painting of lilies the delicacy of their petals is suggested with the translucency of inks. I rendered the more solid vase and the background using thicker, more textured paint.

▼ This detail of *Lilies in Tall Vase* shows how I scraped opaque white over the ink to give a more solid effect.

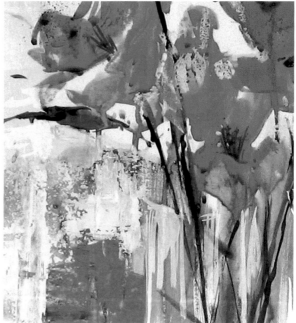

Transparent and opaque colours

In this demonstration, washes of ink provide a tinted background of translucent colour which recedes. The heavier body colours are used for the textured passages in the foreground, the combination of the two creating depth and recession.

MATERIALS USED

25 mm (1 in) synthetic watercolour wash brush

No. 8 round synthetic watercolour brush

12 mm (½ in) flat brush

No. 6 rigger

Mountboard or watercolour paper

Acrylic inks:

Flame Orange

Lemon Yellow

Prussian Blue (Hue)

Heavy body tube colour:

Bright Aqua Green

Burnt Sienna

Burnt Umber

Lemon Yellow

Light Blue Violet

Phthalo Blue (Green Shade)

Titanium White

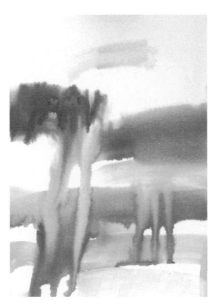

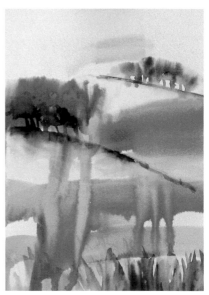

1 Wet the paper with clean water, using your wash brush, then lay Lemon Yellow ink over the whole surface. Apply Flame Orange ink to the middle section and the lower part of the paper in a hit and miss fashion. Allow to dry, or use a hairdryer to speed up the process.

2 Rewet the top right-hand corner and, using your No. 8 round brush, drop Prussian Blue ink onto the wet surface and let it disperse rather than brushing it on. Repeat the same procedure on the left-hand side. Dampen the bottom of the paper and brush in a mix of Prussian Blue and Lemon Yellow inks, dragging the brush up to form leaf shapes in the foreground.

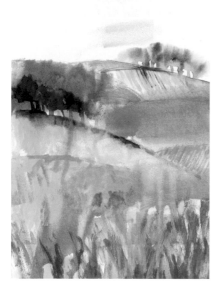

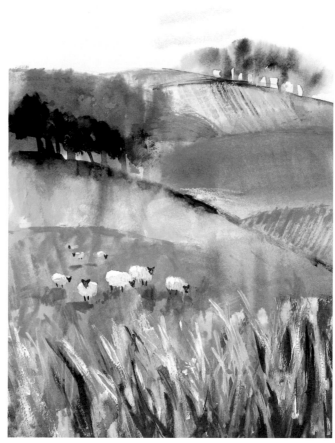

3 In the top right-hand corner beneath the trees, make furrows with Prussian Blue ink. Mix a dark green with Phthalo Blue, Lemon Yellow and Burnt Sienna in thicker paint for the nearer trees and the foreground plants. Scumble Light Blue Violet over the field in the front. Let this dry and scumble a layer of Bright Aqua Green over the same area.

4 Finally, paint the sheep with a mix of Light Blue Violet and Titanium White and apply thicker paint to shape the foliage in the foreground plants.

◀ **Fields with Sheep**
30 × 23 cm (12 × 9 in)

Blending

Blending is the technique of diffusing one area of colour and tone into another. The fast-drying nature of acrylics requires you to act quickly in order to achieve this successfully, but applying a few drops of paint retarder or slow-drying medium will give you slightly more time. The thicker the area of colour the easier the blending process is.

This method is useful for lost and found passages in a painting where you need to lose edges or where gradation of tone is necessary.

▶ **Pomegranate**
20 × 20 cm (8 × 8 in)
Gradation of colour on the skin was necessary to give the fruit its round shape. I blended the colour in the area of highlight and the gradation of darker to lighter tones.

▼ **Grapes**
Several thin layers of Crimson and Purple Lake ink form the individual grapes. In the shadow areas I painted them first with a thin glaze of Ultramarine tube colour in order to make them recede.

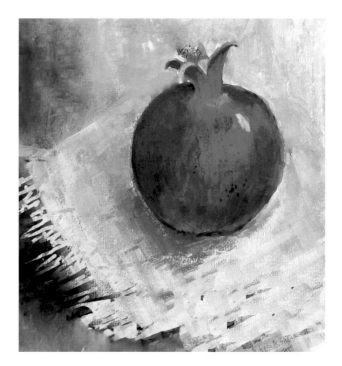

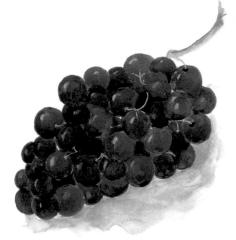

Glazing

Glazing, done by applying multiple thin layers of transparent or semi-transparent colour on top of each other, creates amazing depth and richness of colour. You can also glaze at the latter stages over opaque paint, which is the technique more frequently employed with acrylic pigments. This is especially useful to correct the value or intensity of colour – for example, a warm colour in the background can be glazed with a thin layer of a cooler colour to make it recede. Always allow each layer to dry before applying another one on top.

Scumbling

Scumbling is a technique that comes under the umbrella of 'broken colour'. It means glazing colour by using almost dry semi-transparent or opaque colour on top of another colour, allowing the underlying layers to show through and thus creating a broken colour effect. This method can be used to knock back areas of bright colour and is also quite effective in representing a smoky or hazy atmosphere.

QUICK TIP

Adding either mat or gloss medium to paint increases its transparency and makes it more suitable for glazing.

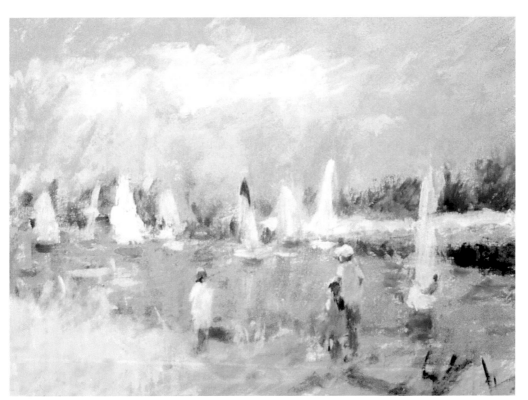

◀ **Children's Boat Race**
20 × 25 cm (8 × 10 in)
In this painting I scumbled Titanium White and Buff Titanium over the sky to form clouds. In the foreground, the same treatment created the feel of a hazy day.

Watercolour and opaque style

Offering a choice of transparent washes of colour, thickly textured applications or a combination of the two, acrylics give the artist greater freedom of expression than any other medium. This project will encourage you to explore their possibilities.

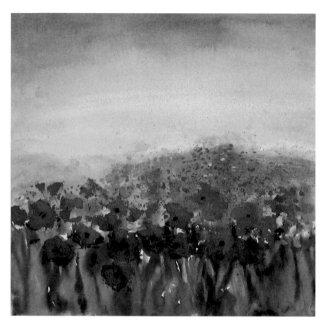

◀ **Poppy Fields**
25 × 25 cm (10 × 10 in)
In this picture I chose to paint the sky and the distant fields in ink washes that make them recede. I applied a combination of watercolour and opaque style to the red poppies and the foliage in the foreground so that some appear to be more distant and others advance.

Experiment with paint

Choose a favourite subject that lends itself to a combination of watercolour and opaque techniques. Try applying washes of transparent colour as the underpainting and allow some of the washes to show through the subsequent layers; the watercolour passages will recede and the heavier-texture areas will come forward, creating depth and recession in the painting.

Another good exercise with acrylics is to paint your subject matter once in the style of watercolour and once using an opaque technique. You can also repeat the same subject, applying different techniques in watercolour such as wet-into-wet or wet-on-dry and a few different opaque techniques such as impasto or scumbling. This very useful exercise will teach you how to judge which style to choose for particular subjects in order to create the maximum impact in your painting.

Finally, choose a subject and start off by applying transparent washes of colour, then go on to add heavier-texture acrylics. Repeat the same subject but this time begin by using heavier-texture acrylics, then change or modify some areas by glazes of transparent colour. This is particularly useful for shadows or toning down areas of bright colours.

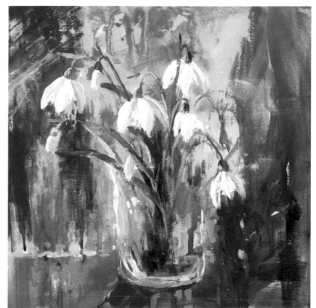

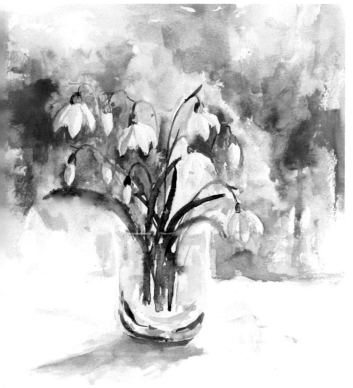

◄ Snowdrops 1
25 × 25 cm (10 × 10 in)
I made a few outlines of the snowdrops to save the white paper for their petals. I applied water around the flowerheads then laid down Coeruleum and Ultramarine in the surrounding area. I added shadow colours to the flowers afterwards.

▲ Snowdrops 2
25 × 25 cm (10 × 10 in)
In contrast to the watercolour style shown left, in this painting I applied opaque Coeruleum and Ultramarine and established a dark background first. I then painted in the darker tones of the flowers before adding the white highlights.

Using other tools

Acrylic paints can be applied using other tools, and each implement will result in a different finish. For example, a roller flattens the colour and the result is totally unlike that of paint laid by a brush. Scraping paint using a credit card is another option – it has a hit and miss effect which allows the layers underneath to show through and make attractive abstract shapes. The edge of the card dipped in ink is also great for drawing straight lines. If you try using various tools, no matter how unlikely they seem, you will enlarge your repertoire of effects.

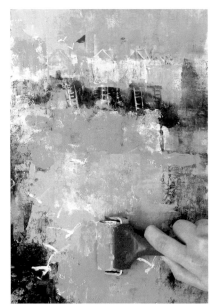

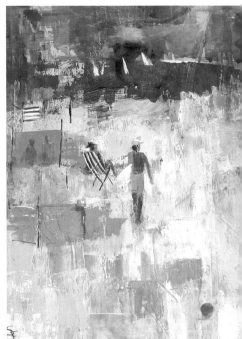

▲ This painting was built up by using a roller, apart from a few brush marks to finish off the beach huts. It was quick, great fun and effective. You must wait for each layer to dry before applying another one.

▶ **The Red Beach Ball**
46 × 35 cm (18 × 14 in)
My technique for this painting was to scrape on a layer of paint with a card, allow it to dry, and then scrape another one on top. I used the edge of the card dipped in paint to depict the straight lines of the wind breakers.

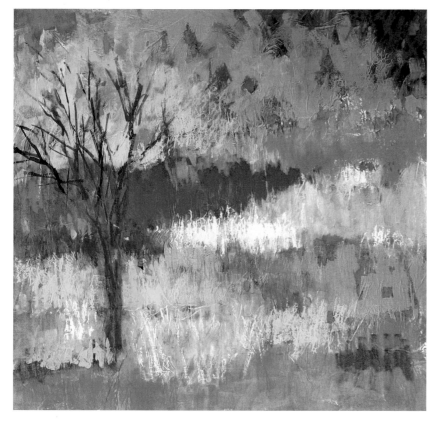

▲ Field Patterns
35 × 35 cm (14 × 14 in)
In this painting I blocked in some colours and shapes first using acrylic colour and then highlighted areas with pastel applied over the top.

Acrylic with other mediums

Acrylic colour makes a very receptive surface on which to apply other mediums. Oil painters have used acrylic as a base for many years. It also makes a great base for oil and soft pastels. Applying a layer of acrylic or acrylic primer (gesso) can create tooth on a smooth card, making it an ideal surface for pastel.

QUICK OVERVIEW

☐ Combine translucent washes with opaque colour for interesting paintings.

☐ Glaze with translucent layers of pigment to add depth and richness to your painting.

☐ Create broken colour either with brush strokes or by scumbling.

☐ Use a variety of tools to apply your paint so that you create different effects.

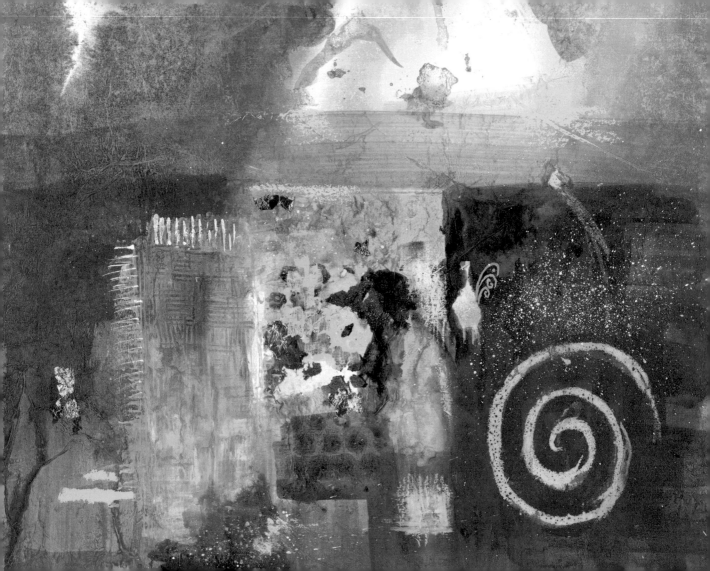

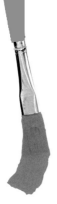

CREATING TEXTURES

The heavy body of acrylic colours makes them ideal for creating textural effects, either for particular surfaces such as grass or stone walls or for abstract or semi-abstract passages within a painting. Super heavy body colours can retain brush strokes or the marks made by a painting knife or other tools, and you can also experiment with a wide variety of texture-making products in combination with the paints.

In this chapter you will discover a few of the many ways in which you can push the boundaries with texture and see how quickly exciting surfaces can be created with this medium.

◀ **Textured Abstract**
24 × 30 cm (9½ × 12 in)
In this painting I have used a variety of materials such as texture paste, tissue paper, splattering and stamp to create texture and pattern.

Using thick acrylic colour

Super heavy body acrylics are the most suited to creating textural effects with paint alone. Use plenty of pigment with very little water so that the paint can retain the brush marks or any other tool that you are using to make texture. A metal brush, comb or painting knife are all ideal to use for this. Grass, stone walls, rocks and animal fur are a few of the possible textures you can suggest with this method.

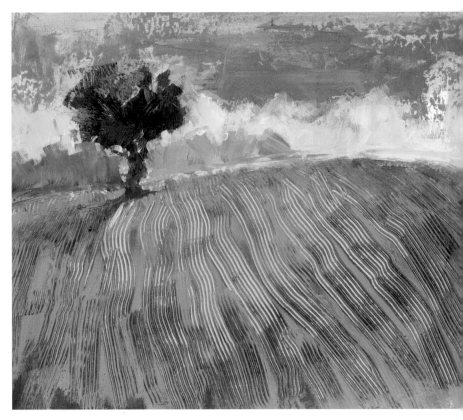

▶ **Furrowed Field**
21 × 26 cm (8½ × 10¼ in)
In this painting I used System 3D Yellow Ochre as a base colour, then painted the field in Burnt Umber. I scratched out the furrows in the field with a metal comb to reveal some of the ochre from underneath.

Using texture paste

You can also choose from a wide range of texture-making products such as texture paste, modelling paste, ceramic stucco, natural sand, glass beads and so forth. For best results apply the paste to your support with a painting knife and create the texture you want, then let it dry completely before you paint on the surface. In a representational landscape, reduce the textural effects towards the background to add to the feeling of recession.

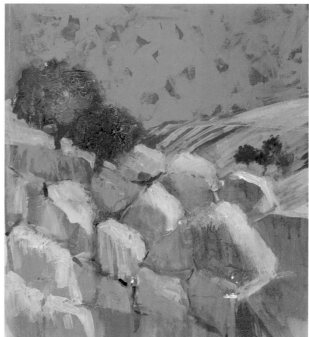

◀ **Rock Patterns**
29 × 26 cm
(11½ × 10¼ in)
I used texture paste to shape the rocks and pressed fabric to the paste on the trees to suggest foliage. I painted the picture mainly with ink.

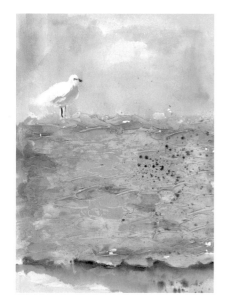

◀ **Seagull on the Stone Wall**
23 × 16 cm (9 × 6½ in)
I used ceramic stucco to create the texture of the stone wall with a fairly small knife, then painted it with a mixture of ink and tube colour.

QUICK TIP

It is much easier to shape the paste with a painting knife, which is also easier to clean afterwards than a brush.

Using simple collage

Using collage on your painting support breaks up the surface, so you no longer have a daunting piece of white paper waiting for your first mark. You can create different textures by using various types of handmade paper, tissue paper, newspaper text, textiles, magic metal (imitation gold leaf) and so on.

Collage is particularly useful if you want to work in a semi-abstract or abstract fashion. You can apply your materials randomly and then manipulate the shapes to suit your subject matter or however you think they might be effective.

▼ **Collage materials**
A selection of collage materials might include tissue paper, handmade paper, leaf skeletons, magic metal and newspaper text.

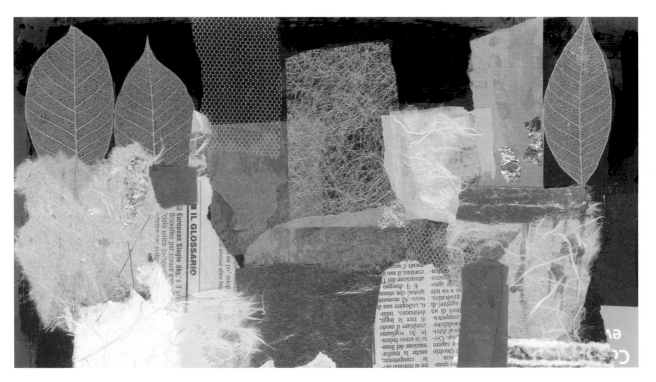

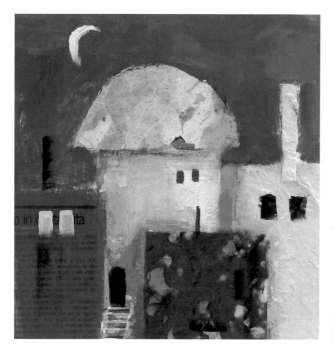

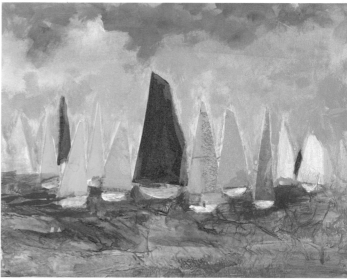

▲ **Greek Buildings**
(detail)
Pieces of handmade
paper and tissue
paper create the
random shapes of
the buildings.
The texture on the
handmade paper
is ideal to suggest
the rough walls
of the building.

▶ **Boat Race**
18 × 25 cm (7 × 10 in)
In this painting,
I used magazine
cut-outs and
coloured paper to
shape the sails
and tissue paper for
the texture in the
sea area.

Exploring different textures

The heavy body of acrylic colours makes them ideal for creating interesting textures. You can manipulate the paint to give texture or add other material to the paint. In this project, let your imagination run wild.

What to do

Find objects that can be used as a tool to make texture on thick paint, such as a metal brush, a comb and so forth. Look also for a variety of objects that can leave an interesting imprint on thick paint or gel medium, such as bubble wrap, fruit netting, metal grid or various types of fabric.

Collect some materials that can be added to the paints to create texture, such as texture paste, modelling paste, natural sand and glass beads. Materials such as tissue paper and handmade paper can be glued to your paper with PVA glue prior to painting to produce a textured ground. Cling film, wax resist, oil pastels, stamps and stencils can all be used successfully with acrylic inks to create interesting effects.

Experiment with texture

Draw 8 × 8 cm (3¼ × 3¼ in) boxes on your paper and experiment with a different type of texture in each square box to build a library of reference materials. Finally, choose a subject on which to try out a few of your textures.

Don't use too many different textures, and balance a busy area with a quiet passage. In a representational painting, keep heavily textured areas in the foreground and reduce texture towards the background to create depth.

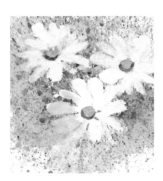

▲ **Spattering**
After masking the daisies, ink was spattered with an old toothbrush to create a textured background.

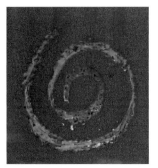

▲ **Wax resist**
The swirl was painted with oil pastel which then resisted the ink wash to great effect.

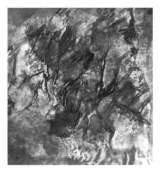

▲ **Tissue paper**
Tissue paper was glued to the surface with PVA then allowed to dry before painting on it.

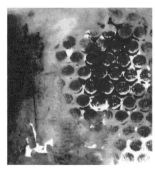

▲ **Bubble wrap**
A piece of bubble wrap pressed on a wash of strong ink left a characteristic imprint.

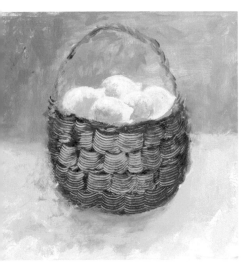

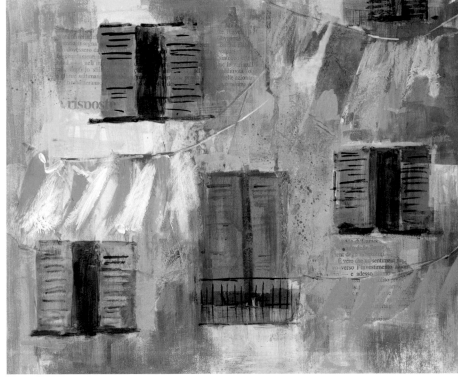

▲ **Basket of Lemons**
20 × 20 cm (8 × 8 in)
After applying a layer
of Yellow Ochre
and letting it dry,
I painted this over
with Burnt Sienna
and used a metal
comb to create the
weave of the basket.

▶ **Washing Line,
Venice**
21 × 25 cm (8 ½ × 10 in)
Here I used natural
sand and newsprint
on the walls, tissue
paper for the clothes
on the line and some
handmade paper on
the shutters.

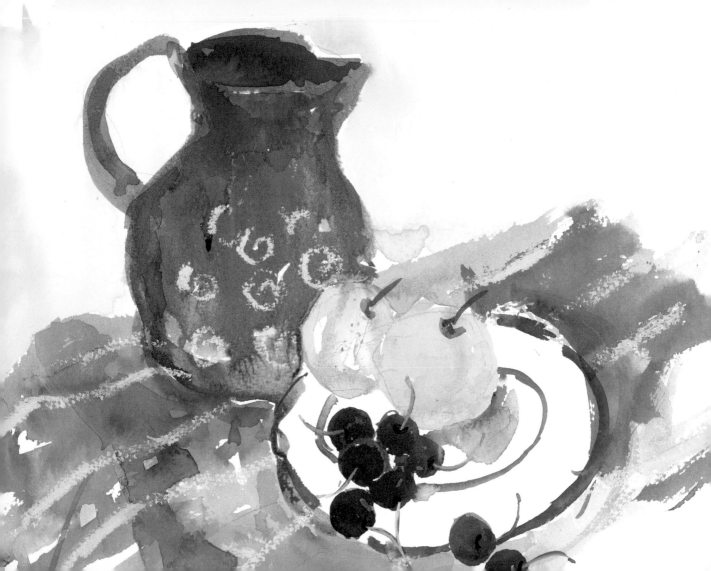

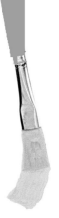

QUICK STUDIES

When you are starting out it is important not to bombard yourself with too many issues at once or you will become overwhelmed. Making quick studies will help you to tackle the individual elements and objects which collectively make a complete painting, so this chapter concentrates on one single idea without the complication of composition and other factors.

These quick little studies can be quite charming and will make a wonderful reference library for you to draw from when attempting bigger, more complex paintings.

◀ **Still Life with Cherries**
21 × 27 cm (8½ × 10½ in)
This quick study of a still life, done with ink and oil pastel, is a reference for a future painting.

Flowers and leaves

Flowers give you the opportunity to play with colour to explore their amazing and intricate forms. To begin with, don't make things difficult for yourself with complicated arrangements – just concentrate on a single bloom.

During the summer months you can fill a whole sketch pad with all the popular cottage garden plants. In time you will come to decide which flower will benefit from being painted with inks in watercolour style, for example red poppies and anemones, and which are best with thick acrylic colour, such as daisies. Some, including sunflowers, are best suited to a combination of the two.

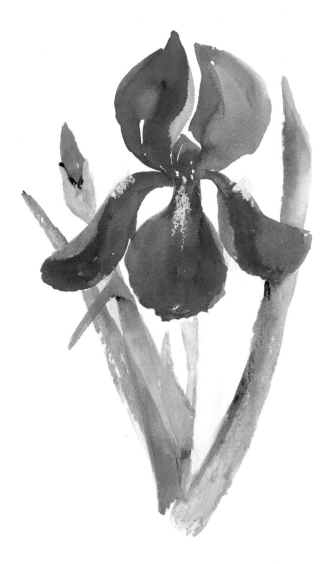

▶ **Iris**
For the iris I used Dioxazine Purple tube colour and some Indigo ink in a combination of thick and thin application. The large petals of iris are great fun to paint. I applied a dab of thick yellow for the centre of the petal.

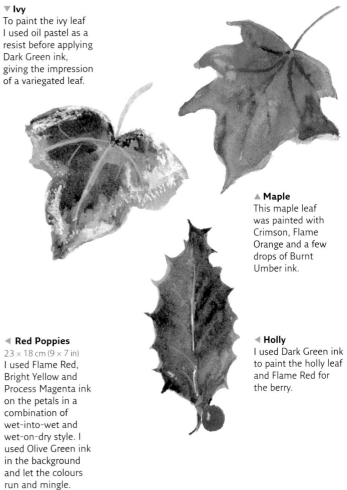

▼ Ivy
To paint the ivy leaf I used oil pastel as a resist before applying Dark Green ink, giving the impression of a variegated leaf.

▲ Maple
This maple leaf was painted with Crimson, Flame Orange and a few drops of Burnt Umber ink.

◀ Holly
I used Dark Green ink to paint the holly leaf and Flame Red for the berry.

◀ Red Poppies
23 × 18 cm (9 × 7 in)
I used Flame Red, Bright Yellow and Process Magenta ink on the petals in a combination of wet-into-wet and wet-on-dry style. I used Olive Green ink in the background and let the colours run and mingle.

Landscape details

Trees play a big part in landscape paintings, so a close observation of the individual shapes of different species and how they grow is quite important. Pay close attention to the shape of the trunk and the overall outline of the tree.

In most landscape paintings it is best to make merely a suggestion of foliage and treat it as a mass rather than painting every leaf. A rigger brush is useful for painting the branches. Details such as fir cones, berries and birds' nests can feature in a small-scale landscape painting but are all interesting subjects on their own too.

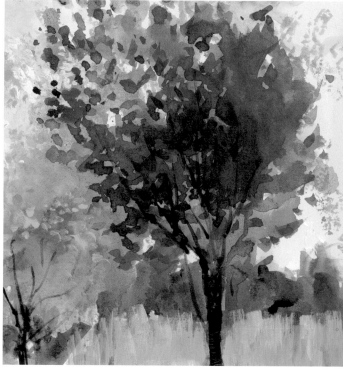

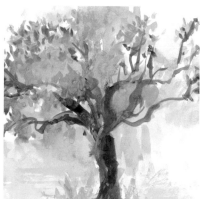

▶ **Olive Tree**
14 × 15 cm (4½ × 6 in)
I love the crooked branches and blue-green pointed leaves of the olive tree. I painted the trunk with thick pigment and used a mixture of green and blue ink for the foliage.

▲ **Copper Beech**
14 × 14 cm (5½ × 5½ in)
Once I had put in the overall shape of the tree, I used numerous dabs of Purple Lake and Crimson ink to suggest the foliage.

▼ Fir Cone
I painted this fir cone with diluted Burnt Umber. Before the paint dried I lifted some colour to shape the scales.

▶ Berries
I used Crimson and Flame Red ink in the glazing method to paint the berries and suggest the round shapes.

▶ Bird's Nest
After using heavy body acrylic to paint the bird's nest I dragged light Yellow Ochre over the dark colour to create the weave of the nest.

Water and boats

Water, with its reflective surface quality, is one of the most challenging subjects for the artist. It mirrors the environment and it is highly affected by the changing light and the climate; a gentle breeze can easily break a mirror reflection into a fractured one in seconds.

The opacity of the pigments, the richness of the colours and the availability of an opaque white makes acrylic an ideal medium for painting waterscapes such as rivers, waterfalls, lakes and the sea.

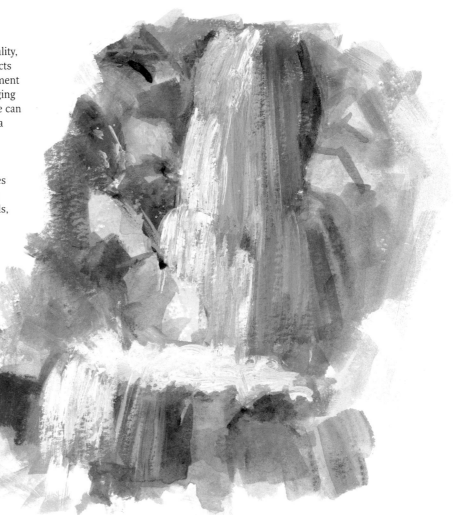

▶ **Waterfall**
16 × 17 cm (6¼ × 6¼ in)
Yellow Ochre and Olive Green inks defined the area surrounding the fall and I applied Indigo underneath it to create a dark background for the water. Finally, I used Titanium White acrylic colour to suggest the water.

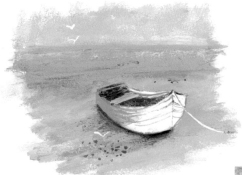

QUICK TIP

In mirror reflections, make the
reflected image darker in value by
glazing a layer of grey-blue wash
over it to soften the image and
make it more convincing.

▲ **Dinghy**
I made a loose
outline of the dinghy
first then used
mainly thick opaque
colour to paint this
little study.

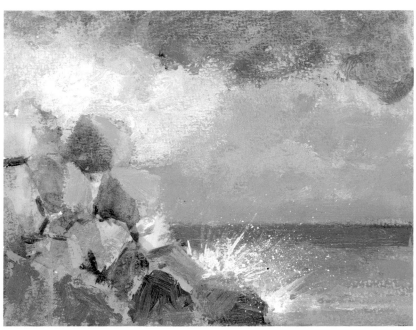

▶ **Sea and Rocks**
10 × 14 cm (4 × 5¾ in)
I used Yellow Ochre
ink to establish the
rocks and painted
the rest of this little
study with tube
colour. I applied white
acrylic ink to suggest
the splash of waves
against the rocks.

Objects

Of all subjects for the artist, inanimate objects are the least problematic; not only are they static, but an interesting range of them can be found in abundance in any home.

Painting a single object, or a few related ones, is good practice for the time when you want to include them in a bigger painting. Their shapes fall into four categories of sphere, cone, cylinder or cube, and they will train your eye for judging the right tonal values and the relationship between different shapes. Items in the kitchen or on the coffee table, however ordinary, make ideal doodling material and great practice for future still life paintings.

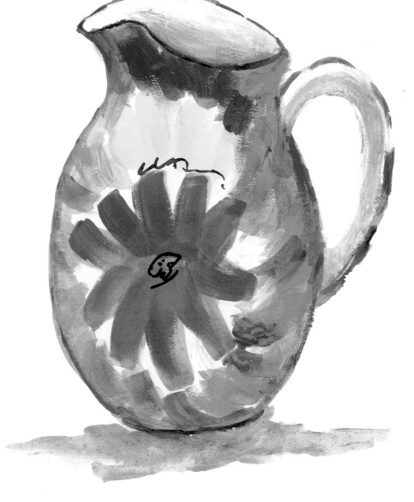

▶ **Spanish Jug**
I used a combination of watercolour and opaque techniques to make a swift painting of this hand-decorated, brightly coloured jug.

▼ Beach Bag and Sun Hat
This simple little study of a beach bag and hat can be incorporated in beach and seaside paintings. I used thick acrylic colour to paint it.

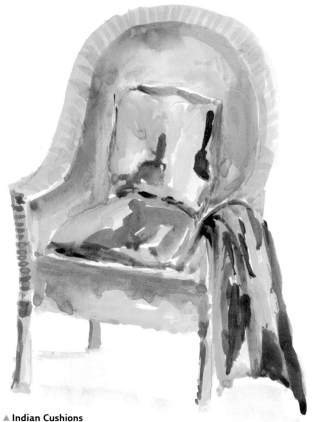

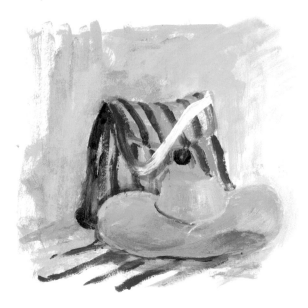

▲ Indian Cushions
For this very quick study of my bedroom chair with its Indian cushions, acrylic inks in watercolour style were ideal.

Animals and birds

Farm animals and wildlife provide a huge range of subject matter for the artist. However, they are difficult to paint from life unless you are an experienced wildlife artist, and this is a time when photographs can be a useful aid, as long as you avoid the trap of just copying them.

Acrylics make an excellent medium for painting animals, as you can establish the overall shape first with diluted colour and then move on to creating different textures of hair, feathers and skin with thicker colours. The vibrant colours of acrylic inks are ideal for painting all manner of colourful birds, butterflies and sea creatures.

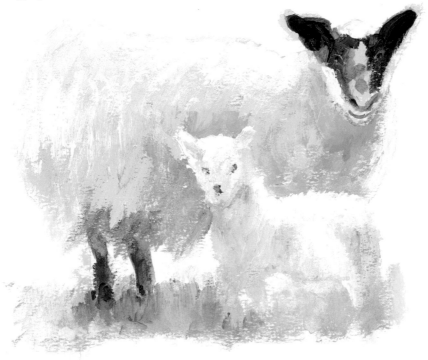

◀ **Mother and Child**
The woolly coat of sheep is best described in thick acrylic colour. I used Unbleached Titanium White, light blue for shadow colours and Titanium White for the highlights.

▶ Parrot

The wonderful bright feathers of parrots are great to paint in acrylic colours. I used Flame Red, Process Cyan and Light Green ink with wet-on-dry technique to paint this bird.

▎QUICK TIP

A comber or fan brush is ideal for depicting animal fur or birds' feathers. Make a light colour wash over the area first then use opaque paint.

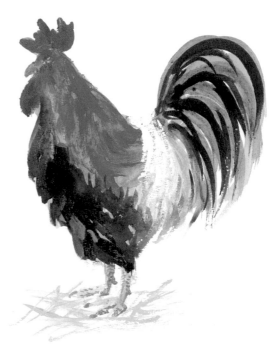

▶ Cockerel

I used a combination of opaque and transparent colours to paint the cockerel; the main body was done in thicker paint and the tail with acrylic inks. Dry brush technique is ideal for feathers, using lots of pigment with very little water.

Figures

The human figure is by far the most challenging of all subjects, but acrylic paint is a great medium for painting it as you can correct any mistakes. Knowing this will give you confidence to go ahead and try, however daunting you may find it.

Although people come in different shapes and sizes, the proportion for the average figure is around 7-7½ heads tall, and to paint convincing figures this proportion needs to be right. Practise by doing many quick little gesture drawings with lots of energy and movement, so that when you come to include figures in your compositions you can draw from this experience. If there is a local life drawing class you can attend it will not only help you with figure painting but improve your drawing skills generally.

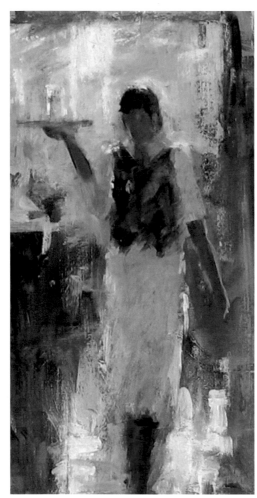

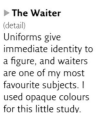

▶ The Waiter
(detail)
Uniforms give immediate identity to a figure, and waiters are one of my most favourite subjects. I used opaque colours for this little study.

▼ Girl by the Sea
Although the figure is standing still, the feeling of movement through the hair and the skirt stops it being totally static. I used a combination of thick and diluted colour for this figure.

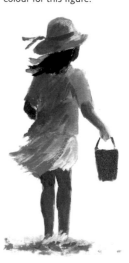

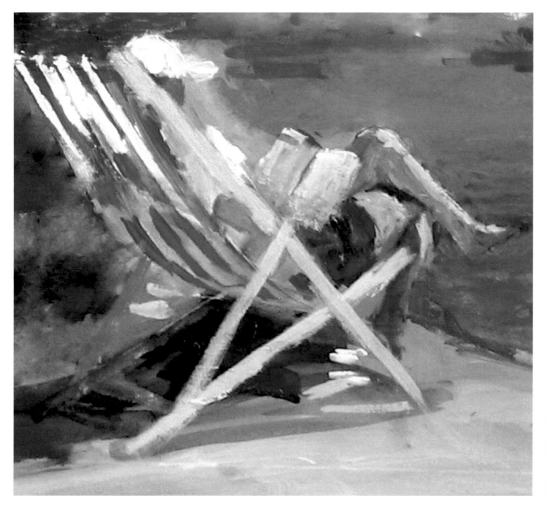

◀ **Deckchair**
(detail)
For this painting
I used thick colour.
The figure is facing
away from us, which
makes it a bit more
intriguing.

▼ **Tuscany Villas**
10 × 23 cm (4 × 9 in)
Buildings that are of different height and appearance make a more interesting arrangement than uniform ones. I used some Yellow Ochre ink to give an overall warm glow to the buildings and Dark Green ink on the foliage of the surrounding trees.

Buildings

Perspective is the most challenging aspect of painting architectural subjects. If the focal point of your painting is the buildings, perspective should be carefully considered. If this is something you find difficult, simplifying the buildings will usually make it less problematic.

Start by straightforward subjects such as a doorway or a windowbox before tackling entire buildings. In the case of a complicated building, try not to paint every window and leave some of the details to the imagination of the viewer. Once again the opacity of acrylics will come to the rescue should you make any errors as you can easily correct them.

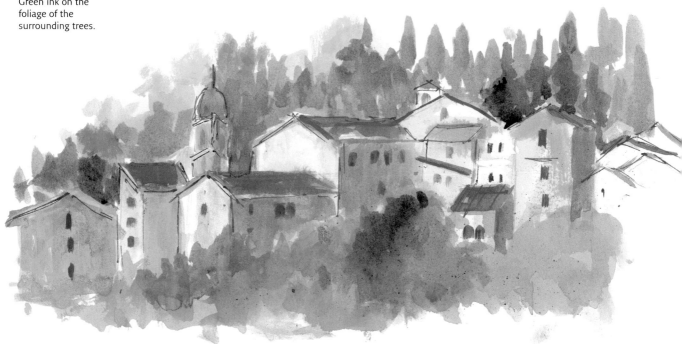

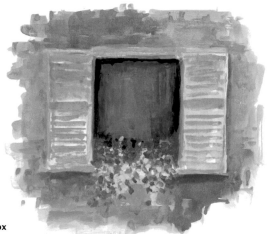

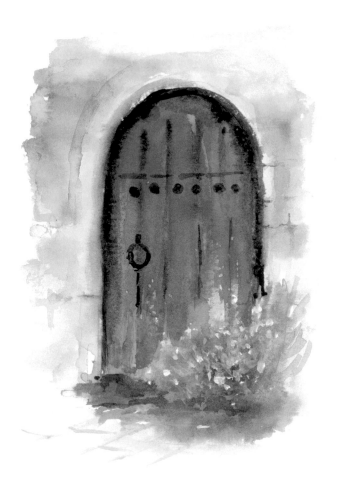

**▶ French
Windowbox**
18 × 20 cm (7 × 8 in)
Details of buildings
such as windows
and doorways make
interesting subject
matter. This
windowbox was
painted mainly with
acrylic inks.

◀ Old Doorway
20 × 15 cm (8 × 6 in)
Attractive old
doorways make
lovely subjects. I
applied several glazes
of Burnt Umber and
Red Earth ink to
paint the door and
spread the ink
further to the
surrounding area.

QUICK OVERVIEW

☐ To begin with, concentrate on a
single element within a range of
different subjects.

☐ Paint variations on a single idea, such
as different species of flowers or trees.

☐ Make a useful reference library of
these to include in future paintings.

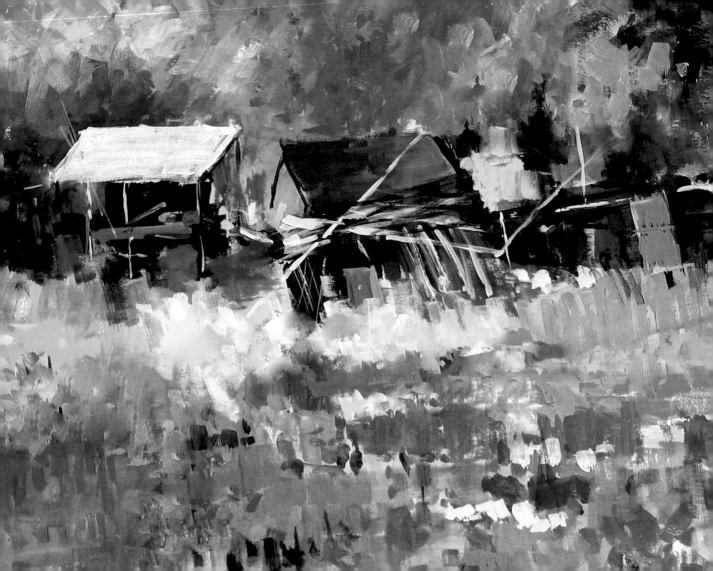

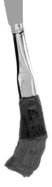

COMPOSING YOUR PICTURE

Composition is the framework upon which your subject matter is built. A good composition will attract the viewer and hold their attention; a bad one can make the painting at best simply boring and at worst visually disturbing.

This chapter covers a few fundamental elements regarding composition. While the experienced artist is able to break all the rules and get away with it, if you are a beginner it is best to stick to these guidelines as they will help you to create a more integrated and dynamic painting.

◄ **Derelict Barns**
35 × 41 cm (14 × 16 in)
In this composition the emphasis is on the foreground, with the buildings creating the busy part of the picture.

Compositional rules

Following the tips given here will help you make interesting and balanced compositions. Your aim is to lead the viewer's eye round the painting and to create a point of main focus.

▪ Simplify your reference material and eliminate any unnecessary or unwanted detail that exists.

▪ Divide your picture space into unequal segments, and vary the proportion and importance of objects.

▪ Follow the rule of thirds (see below).

▪ In landscapes, have a large area of either sky or land – do not place the horizon line in the middle as this cuts the painting in half.

▪ In aerial perspective, warm colours come forward and cooler colours recede. Use this to create depth in your painting.

▪ In still lifes, overlap the objects rather than placing them side by side so that they just touch.

▪ Compose the picture with attention to the tonal values as well as the elements within the subject.

▪ Lead the eye into your painting with linear elements such as paths and walls.

▪ Make odd numbers of key elements, for example three sheep rather than two in a landscape.

▪ Pay careful attention to the negative spaces around the subject. These are just as important to the composition as the positive shapes and need to be just as interesting.

▪ The introduction of too many isolated figures divides the focus of interest, with each one vying for the viewer's attention. Grouping some of the figures together and balancing them with a few strategically placed single figures makes a better composition.

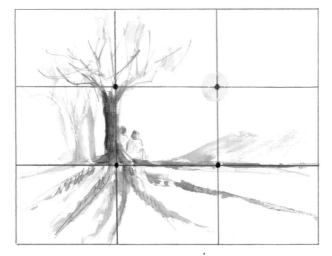

▶ Divide your paper into thirds vertically and horizontally. Each intersection of the dividing lines makes a suitable area for the focal point of your painting (known as the rule of thirds).

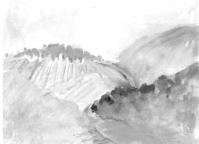

▲ Devise ways of leading the viewer's eye into and through the painting.

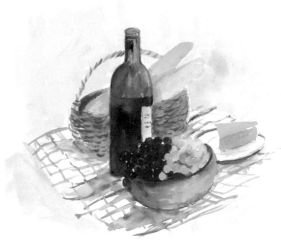

▲ **A French Picnic**
25 × 30 cm (10 × 12 in)
In this still life the
objects relate to
each other; they are
grouped together
to make a more
dynamic composition.

◀ **Summer Fields**
25 × 25 cm (10 × 10 in)
This painting is
about the texture
of the field in the
foreground. By
having a smaller sky
I have avoided cutting
the painting in half.

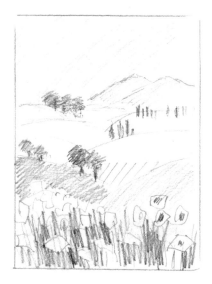

▲ This is the thumbnail sketch I made for *Provence Landscape* (opposite) while I was working out whether to have a portrait or landscape format.

▶ In this second sketch I tried the landscape format, but decided that I liked the portrait format better.

Thumbnail sketches

Don't plan to fail by failing to plan! Thumbnail sketches are the most efficient way of planning for a painting. These are small, roughly drawn sketches where you invest just a few minutes to work out the structure of your painting.

In your sketch pad, draw four or five small boxes the same shape as your paper or canvas. Within this small format, you can simplify the subject matter, work out your tonal values, compose your picture and decide on a landscape, portrait or square format. A little planning goes a long way to avoid frustration at a later stage and to help you make a better painting.

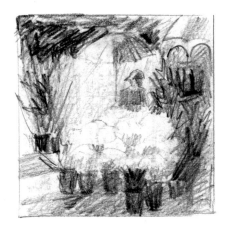

▲ In this quick little sketch for *Flower Market* (see p.93) I have blocked in all my shapes and tonal values.

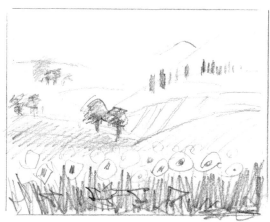

Using an underpainting

Making an underpainting has several advantages, not least that it banishes the whiteness of paper or canvas which some artists find most disconcerting. It can be used to set a certain mood or ambience for the whole picture – an underpainting of cool greys and blues is ideal for painting a rainy day, for example. You can also use underpainting to block in your darks, lights and mid-tones before you paint any details of the composition.

Underpainting does not have to be in monochrome; a colourful underpainting which shows through subsequent layers can create quite a visual feast. Underpainting in complementary colours can create strong visual contrasts – where you have areas of foliage try using red as underpainting, or apply orange as an underpainting for the blue of the sea. With acrylic colours you have the option of using a combination of thick and diluted paint or washes of ink to create transparent passages which will recede and add depth.

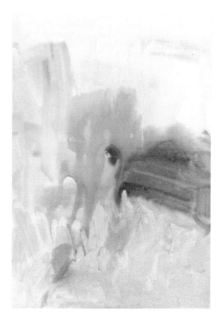

▲ I used a cool and warm yellow as an underpainting for *Provence Landscape* with a dash of orange to give a sunny feel.

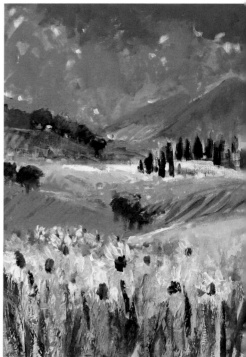

▶ **Provence Landscape**
30 × 25 cm (12 × 10 in)
Allowing the yellow underpainting to show through the top layers provides harmony and cohesion within the whole painting as well as creating a sunny ambience.

Underpainting

In this demonstration, Ultramarine underpainting helps to create the darker values of the colours that will be applied on top. The Lemon Yellow gives a sunny glow to the background and the lighter sides of the apples, and by letting it show through the subsequent layers uniformity and harmony are created in the painting.

MATERIALS USED

Short flat brushes
  Nos 4, 6, 8
Round brushes
  Nos 2, 4
Daler-Rowney
  Langton 300 gsm
  (140 lb) Not paper
Bright Green

Burnt Sienna
Cadmium Red
Lemon Yellow
Light Blue Violet
Quinacridone Deep
  Purple
Titanium White
Ultramarine

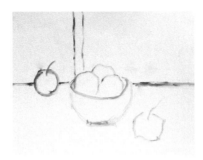

1 Using Ultramarine and a No. 4 round brush, sketch out the basic plan, using a diagonal composition which will lead the viewer's eye from the red apple at top left to rest on the green apple at the bottom.

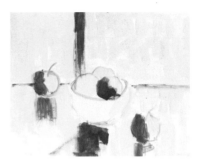

2 Apply an underpainting of Lemon Yellow to give an overall sunny feel to the background and the light streaming through the window. Using Ultramarine, block in some of the darker values.

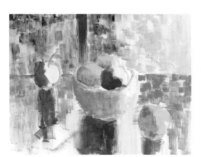

3 Apply Ultramarine to the top left-hand side to suggest a darker area and Bright Green to the right-hand side to show lighter foliage and to the green apples. Paint the windowsill with Light Blue Violet and the window pane with a neutral grey.

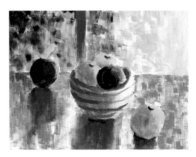

4 Paint the red apples with Quinacridone Deep Purple and a touch of Cadmium Red, leaving the sunlit side lighter. Using Ultramarine and Burnt Sienna, put in the stalks. Use random brushstrokes to suggest foliage in the background.

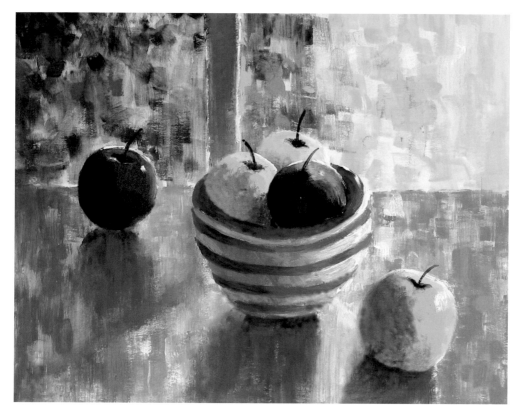

◀ **Apples on a Windowsill**
23 × 25 cm (9 × 10 in)

5 Give the red apples more form and definition with a few glazes of Quinacridone Deep Purple and Cadmium Red and use Bright Green in the case of the green apples. The yellow and blue underpainting helps a great deal with establishing tone in the first place. Strengthen the shadows under the objects and add lighter tones to the windowsill. Finally, paint the stalks and add highlights to finish the picture.

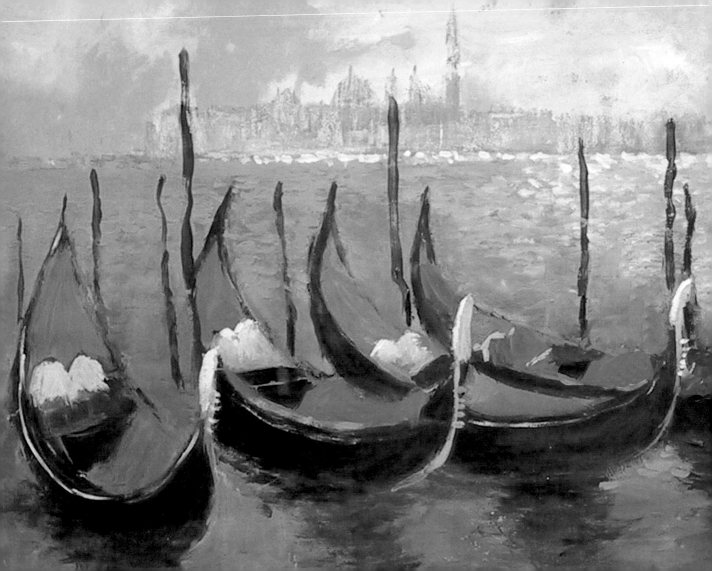

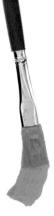

THE COMPLETE PICTURE

By this stage you should be ready to tackle a complete painting. In this chapter there are a few suggestions, but ultimately, as an artist you will find your own thoughts and ideas. After all, a huge part of the fun is gathering information, processing ideas and seeing them to fruition.

There is great joy to be had when things go to plan, but they won't always do so. However, don't be disheartened by failures along the way – regard them as stepping stones to help you towards your goal of achieving successful paintings in just 30 minutes.

◀ **Gondolas**
28 × 38 cm (11 × 15 in)
Here the subtle colour of the distant buildings contrasts with the dark of the gondolas to add depth to the painting.

Landscapes

The sheer scale of the great outdoors can
be quite overwhelming for the beginner,
particularly if you have only limited
time in which to paint. A viewfinder is
a great tool for narrowing down sections
that may interest you; to make one,
just cut an aperture of the appropriate
shape in a piece of card. Hold it up in
front of you and look at the landscape
through it to judge what might make a
pleasing composition.

If there are too many details, simplify
them, and remember that you don't have
to paint what is there – an ugly building
or some feature that doesn't suit your
composition can be omitted. Every
landscape you paint will help to train
your visual and observational skills,
which are just as important as your
technical abilities, if not more so. Seeing
the world through an artist's eye is a
joyful experience.

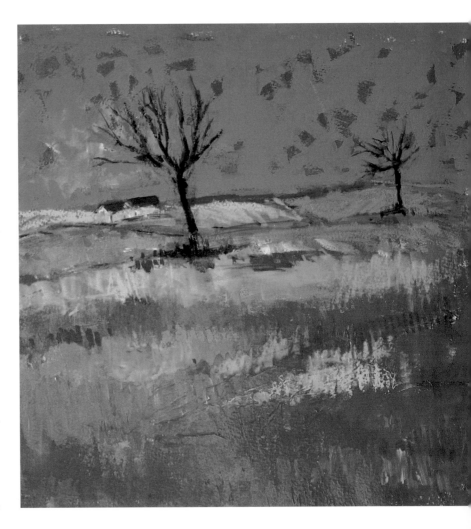

▶**The Red
Landscape**
35 × 35 cm (14 × 14 in)
The hot colours of
this landscape were
inspired by the red
poppy fields of the
summer. I used
mainly tube colour
to paint this picture.

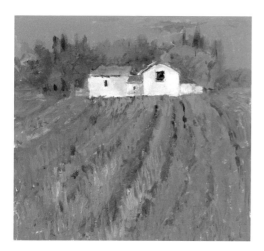

▲ Lavender Fields, Tuscany
25 × 26 cm (10 × 10¼ in)
The perspective of these fields really appealed to me. I used heavy body pigments for this picture, and made a few different shades of cool and warm purples to paint it.

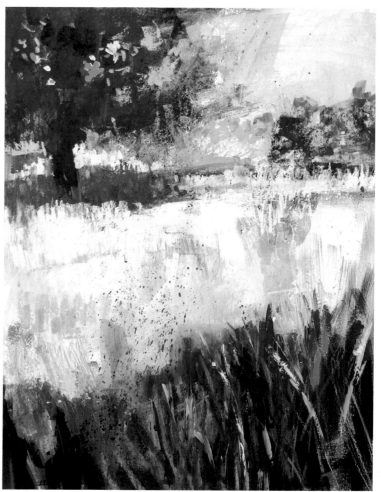

▶ Cornfield
38 × 30 cm (15 × 12 in)
I liked the contrast of light and dark with the tree and the foreground against the cornfield. I used System 3D Yellow Ochre mixed with white in the foreground, with dabs of Cadmium Red to provide accents of colour.

Still life

Still life is one area of painting where the artist has complete control over the design element of the work. It is a great discipline for the artist as it accustoms the eye to judging tonal values and the relationship between different shapes. Directional light from one side or back lighting makes a more dramatic and interesting composition, and the tonal values are very clear to read. A still life is also a good subject for a painting in 30 minutes if you don't have enough time to go out and about.

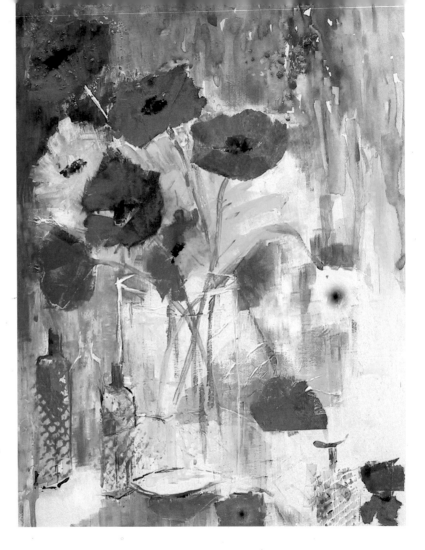

▶ **Still Life with Anemones**
35 × 30 cm (14 × 12 in)
I painted this still life with a combination of inks and thicker colour. I used some torn pieces of tissue paper as collage for textural effect.

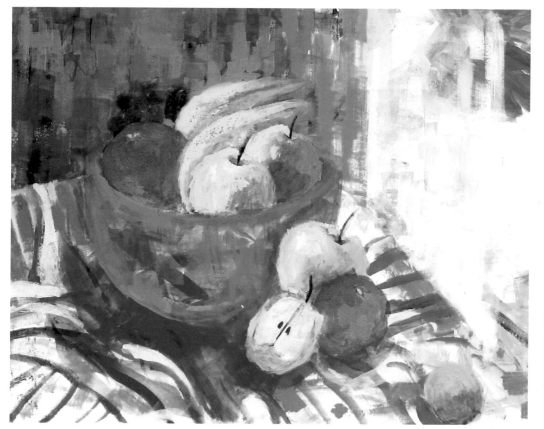

◄ Still Life with Fruit
30 × 41 cm (12 × 16 in)
First I made an underpainting of yellow, blue, magenta and a touch of orange. I used a spot light to illuminate the subject from the left-hand side and added highlights to the painting accordingly.

Water

A vast area of our planet is covered in water, and in its many and varied forms it offers the artist a whole range of opportunity. Harbours and marinas are particularly interesting, with the inclusion of buildings, boats and people.

The colour of water varies a great deal, ranging from the deep blues, purples and turquoise of tropical seas to the deep greens and muddy browns of rivers and stagnant ponds. It is highly changeable according to the season, the weather and the time of the day, and needs careful observation in order to paint it in a convincing way.

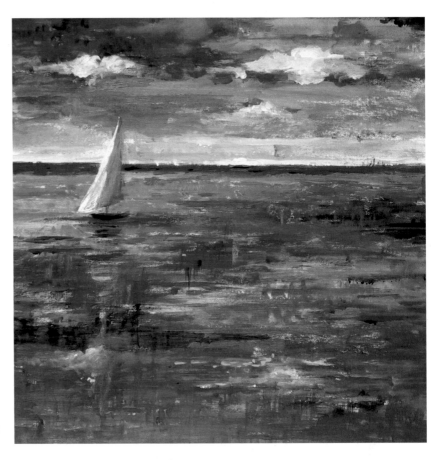

▶ **Tranquillity**
28 × 28 cm (11 × 11 in)
I used rich colour to create the amazing skies. The late afternoon sun catching the sail of the boat makes a good contrast against the dark colours.

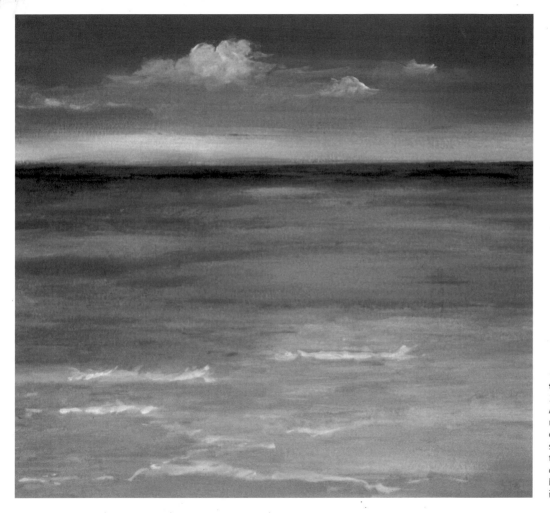

◄ **Colours of the Caribbean**
38 × 41 cm (15 × 16 in)
Acrylic colour really lends itself to depicting subjects such as this, where the gradation of colour from deepest blue to turquoise is necessary.

Urban landscapes

Cityscapes and townscapes often include people as well as buildings, both of which have some challenging issues for the artist. It's best to tackle these elements individually before attempting a complicated cityscape. In your initial paintings, make the buildings more important than the people and vice versa.

All the horizontal parallel lines of the buildings will appear to converge at a single point on the horizon line, which is at your eye level. The size of your figures should be smaller as they get further away, but in the case of adults their heads should remain at the same height.

▶ **New York Buildings**
20 × 10 cm (8 × 4 in)
I chose a very small section of the complicated New York skyline and treated it as simple geometric shapes using a single colour. I then added shadow colour in order to give dimension and suggested windows to bring the buildings to life.

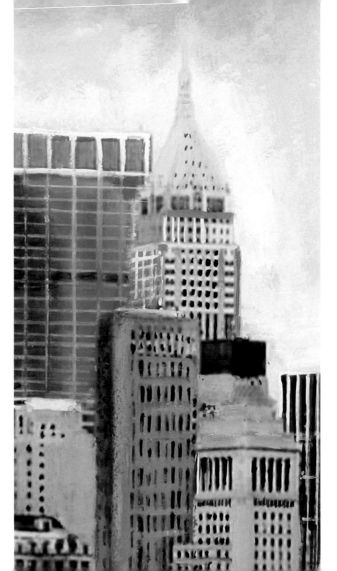

◀ **Greek Island**
(detail)
This is a collage of some of my favourite Greek buildings. I have simplified what was a very busy harbour into shapes and forms that are typical of Greece.

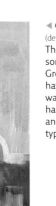

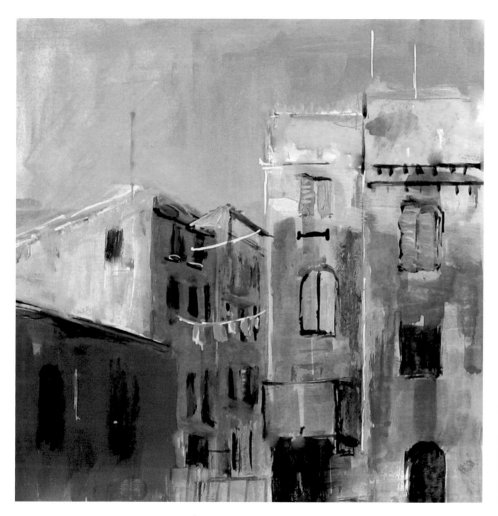

◀ **Venice**
20 × 20 cm (8 × 8 in)
These Venetian
buildings were
comparatively
simple in terms of
perspective. I used
a combination of
transparent and
opaque pigment.

Figures in the landscape

Figures add scale to a landscape and animate the picture. To make them convincing you must get the proportions of the figures right – common mistakes such as drooping shoulders, short arms and large heads can make figures appear wooden and static. Of course you also need to make sure they are in proportion to the landscape features around them.

Eliminate unnecessary detail and suggest figures with a few broad brush strokes to create movement and energy. In crowd scenes, pick a few key figures that interact by facing them towards each other. A painting that includes figures will convey a whole range of moods and emotions to the viewer.

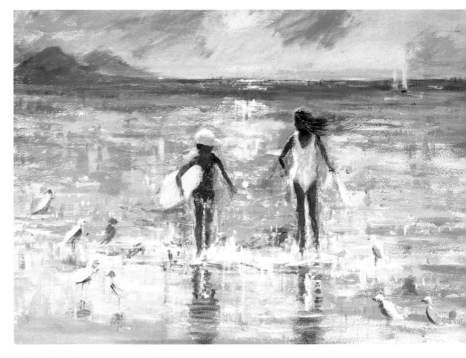

▲ **Body Boarding**
45 × 56 cm (18 × 22 in)
In this painting there is a lot of movement expressed by both the figures and the seagulls. I used broken colour with layers of different blues and purples in order to break up the surface of the sea. After laying a wash of ink initially, I used thick colour thereafter.

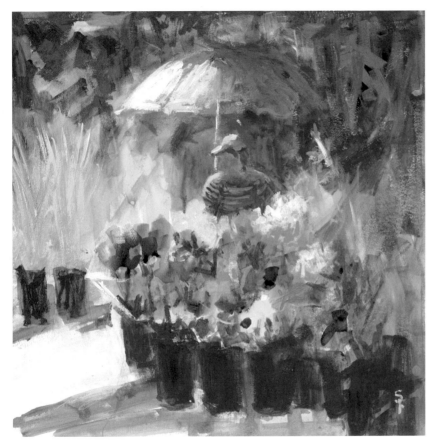

◄ Flower Market

28 × 28 cm (11 × 11 in)

I liked the drama of
light and dark in this
picture, and blocked
in the tonal values
in dark purple, blue
and green. The area
of flowers was
suggested with
dabs of colour with
minimal amount
of detail.

QUICK OVERVIEW

☐ Look through a viewfinder to scale
down an area of interest in a landscape.

☐ Use the effect of light and dark to add
drama to your painting.

☐ Simplify urban landscapes, making
figures or buildings the main subject.

FURTHER INFORMATION

Here are some organizations or resources that you might find useful to help you to develop your painting.

Art Magazines

The Artist, Caxton House, 63/65 High Street, Tenterden, Kent TN30 6BD; tel: 01580 763673 www.theartistmagazine.co.uk
Artists & Illustrators, 26-30 Old Church Street, London SW3 5BY; tel: 020 7349 3150 www.aimag.co.uk
International Artist, P. O. Box 4316, Braintree, Essex CM7 4QZ; tel: 01371 811345 www.artinthemaking.com
Leisure Painter, Caxton House, 63/65 High Street, Tenterden, Kent TN30 6BD; tel: 01580 763315 www.leisurepainter.co.uk

Art Materials

Daler-Rowney Ltd, P. O. Box 10, Bracknell, Berkshire RG12 8ST; tel: 01344 461000 www.daler-rowney.com

T. N. Lawrence & Son Ltd, 208 Portland Road, Hove, West Sussex BN3 5QT; tel: 0845 644 3232 or 01273 260260 www.lawrence.co.uk
Winsor & Newton, Whitefriars Avenue, Wealdstone, Harrow, Middlesex HA3 5RH; tel: 020 8427 4343 www.winsornewton.com

Art Shows

Affordable Art Fair, The Affordable Art Fair Ltd, Unit 3 Heathmans Road, London SW6 4TJ; tel: 020 7371 8787 www.affordableartfair.co.uk
Art in Action, Waterperry House, Waterperry, Nr Wheatley, Oxfordshire OX33 1JZ; tel: 020 7381 3192 (for information) www.artinaction.org.uk
Patchings Art, Craft & Design Festival, Patchings Art Centre, Patchings Farm, Oxton Road, Calverton, Nottinghamshire NG14 6NU; tel: 0115 965 3479 www.patchingsartcentre.co.uk

Art Societies

National Acrylic Painters' Association, 134 Rake Lane, Wallasey, Wirral, Merseyside CH45 1JW; tel: 0151 639 2980 www.napauk.org
Society for All Artists (SAA), P. O. Box 50, Newark, Nottinghamshire NG23 5GY; tel: 01949 844050 www.saa.co.uk

Bookclubs for Artists

Artists' Choice, P. O. Box 3, Huntingdon, Cambridgeshire PE28 0QX; tel: 01832 710201 www.artists-choice.co.uk
Painting for Pleasure, Brunel House, Newton Abbot, Devon TQ12 4BR; tel: 0870 44221223 www.readersunion.co.uk

Internet Resources

Art Museum Network: the official website of the world's leading art museums www.amn.org
Artcourses: an easy way to find part-time classes, workshops and painting holidays in Britain and Europe www.artcourses.co.uk

The Arts Guild: on-line bookclub devoted to books on the art world
www.artsguild.co.uk
British Arts: useful resource to help you to find information about all art-related matters
www.britisharts.co.uk
British Library Net: comprehensive A-Z resource including 24-hour virtual museum/gallery
www.britishlibrary.net/museums.html
Galleries: the UK's largest-circulating monthly art listings magazine, with details of exhibitions and other art services
www.artefact.co.uk
Galleryonthenet: provides member artists with gallery space on the internet
www.galleryonthenet.org.uk
Jackson's Art Supplies: on-line store and mail order company for art materials
www.jacksonsart.com
Open College of the Arts: an open-access college, offering home-study courses to students worldwide
www.oca-uk.com
Painters Online: interactive art club run by The Artist's Publishing Company
www.painters-online.com

Soraya French: the author's website, with details of her exhibitions and workshops, and a gallery of her paintings
www.sorayafrench.com
WWW Virtual Library: extensive information on galleries worldwide
www.comlab.ox.ac.uk/archive/other/museums/galleries.html

Videos

APV Films, 6 Alexandra Square, Chipping Norton, Oxfordshire OX7 5HL;
tel: 01608 641798
www.apvfilms.com
Teaching Art, P. O. Box 50, Newark, Nottinghamshire NG23 5GY;
tel: 01949 844050
www.teachingart.com

FURTHER READING

Why not have a look at other art instruction titles from Collins?

Bellamy, David, *Painting Wild Landscapes in Watercolour*
Blockley, Ann, *Watercolour Textures*
Cambridge, Melanie, *You Can Paint Acrylics*

Crawshaw, Alwyn, *Alwyn Crawshaw's Ultimate Painting Course*
Learn to Paint Acrylics
Jennings, Simon, *Collins Artist's Colour Manual*
Collins Complete Artist's Manual
King, Ian, *Gem Watercolour Tips*
Reiter, Laura, *Learn to Paint Abstracts*
Shepherd, David, *Painting with David Shepherd*
Simmonds, Jackie, *Gem Sketching*
Soan, Hazel, *Gem 10-minute Watercolours*
Secrets of Watercolour Success
Trevena, Shirley, *Vibrant Watercolours*
Waugh, Trevor, *Winning with Watercolour*
Whitton, Judi, *Loosen up your Watercolours*

For further information about Collins books visit our website:
www.collins.co.uk

INDEX